THE

BEST

AMERICAN

POETRY

1994

◊　◊　◊

A. R. Ammons, Editor

David Lehman, Series Editor

A TOUCHSTONE BOOK

PUBLISHED BY SIMON & SCHUSTER

NEW YORK · LONDON · TORONTO · SYDNEY · TOKYO · SINGAPORE

TOUCHSTONE
Rockefeller Center
1230 Avenue of the Americas
New York, New York 10020

Manufactured in the United States of America

1 3 5 7 9 10 8 6 4 2

ISBN 0-671-89948-1 PB
ISSN 1040-5763

CONTENTS

David Lehman was born in New York City in 1948. He graduated from Columbia College in 1970 and attended Cambridge University in England as a Kellett Fellow from 1970 to 1972. Two collections of his poems, *An Alternative to Speech* (1986) and *Operation Memory* (1990), were published by Princeton University Press. His prose books include *Signs of the Times: Deconstruction and the Fall of Paul de Man* (Poseidon Press, 1991) and *The Perfect Murder* (The Free Press, 1989). *The Line Forms Here* appeared in the University of Michigan Press's Poets on Poetry Series in 1992. Lehman is on the core faculty of the low-residency graduate writing program at Bennington College, and has taught at Columbia and at the New School for Social Research. In 1990 he received an award in literature from the American Academy of Arts and Letters, and a year later won a three-year writer's award from the Lila Wallace–Reader's Digest Fund.

FOREWORD

by David Lehman

◇ ◇ ◇

One of the few persons associated with the Clinton administration whose stock has never stopped rising is the poet Maya Angelou, who presented her Inaugural Ode with all the splendor of ceremony on January 20, 1993. Not everyone thought "On the Pulse of Morning" was a wonderful poem, but it was good theater and shrewd politics. Ms. Angelou rhymed *Sioux* and *Jew*, *Greek* and *Sheik*, sweetly opposed war and "cynicism," and ended wishing everyone "good morning." People were deeply moved by her performance. The novelist Louise Erdrich enthusiastically declared she "felt that this woman could have read the side of a cereal box," which was meant to be a compliment though it sort of backfires when you realize that it compares the Inaugural Ode to the side of a cereal box. Erdrich's point, however, was that Angelou's presence was "powerful and momentous." And so it was for most of the thousands in attendance and the millions watching on TV. It's safe to say that the Inaugural was the best-attended poetry reading of the decade. The boost to Ms. Angelou's market value was immediate. *Wouldn't Take Nothing for My Journey Now*, her latest book of essays, quickly made it onto the best-seller list. Half the colleges in the country would give almost anything to have her grace their commencement exercises. The poet has become a symbol of unity in multicultural diversity, and a national role model for young African-American women.

In the road movie *Poetic Justice*, released in the summer of 1993, Janet Jackson gets to write, and recite, the poems of Maya Angelou—which I cite as evidence not only of Ms. Angelou's personal ascendancy but of the current unanticipated prestige that surrounds poetry generically in the culture at large. Verse has suddenly become ubiquitous. There are poems on placards for straphangers to ponder in New York City's buses and subway trains: I've spotted works by Charles Reznikoff, Gwendolyn Brooks, Robert Frost, and William Carlos Williams. Out West, cowboy poetry festivals, like the one held annually in Elko, Nevada, proclaim that a major revival of cowboy verse is in progress. In Beverly Hills the actor Mickey Rourke recently cleared sixteen thousand dollars on the sale of eight framed, poster-size poems he had written. For example: "I Should Have Been Born/A Statue of Stone,/I'd Have No Pain/No Place to Call Home." In Florida, poetry enabled a skillful defense attorney named Roy Black to get his client, a Miami cop, acquitted in a widely publicized murder trial concluding on Memorial Day weekend. Mr. Black moved the jury—and caused his client to weep—when he declaimed a poem, which he characterized as an anonymous policeman's soliloquy, most of which he lifted from chapter sixty-two of *Blue Truth*, a detective novel by a maverick ex-cop from Fort Lauderdale named Cherokee Paul McDonald. A paragraph: "When you were violated, I was violated. When you were dying on the hard pavement, I knelt over you to keep the sun from your eyes. I wore your powerful tin badge on my chest, and it gave me reason. I took out my sword and hurled myself against those who had hurt you."

When Elizabeth Holtzman, the former comptroller of the city of New York, faced defeat in the Democratic senatorial primary, she gamely tried to rally her supporters by quoting this grotesque image from a Marge Piercy poem: "A strong woman is a woman who is straining./A strong woman is a woman standing/On tiptoe and lifting a barbell/While trying to sing Boris Godunov." (No wonder she lost.) *The New York Times* put it on the front page. Not to be outdone, the *New York Post* treated its readers to a tabloid seminar on geek verse: a two-page spread on the terrible teenage poems written by Joel Rifkin, the accused slayer of seventeen prostitutes.

About all this we are entitled to feel at least a little ambivalent. There is the question of quality. People who love poetry, this poorly paid nonprofession, love it so much they hate to see it adulterated, and surely much of the poetry in the news in 1993 was adulterated verse, trite, forgettable, bogus. The Gap commercial with Max Blagg's elegy for his blue jeans, the unkempt bards of downtown bars who became the overnight darlings of the media, the poems of MTV—these may all be events in the history of publicity, rather than that of poetry.

Even so, such developments may have a heartening effect on

those of us who never doubted that American poetry is healthier and more vital, fresher and more various than it is alleged to be. It is good to have that feeling confirmed in the wider populace. But if the world of poetry is spacious enough to accommodate the spurious as well as the genuine article, and if it is only to be expected that exuberance and delight are dealt out in ampler portions than is lasting talent, the need to make critical discriminations has never been greater. And in the absence of reliable, disinterested, intellectually strenuous criticism of poetry, much of this function must be performed by anthologies.

That is one rationale for *The Best American Poetry*, now seven editions strong. Each year a different guest editor chooses seventy-five poems from the year's literary magazines. This is implicitly an act of criticism as well as of celebration. The anthology is frankly elitist in that we hope to honor the poems of our moment that are worthiest of attention and acclaim. At the same time there is a decidedly populist cast to our enterprise since we who collaborate on it try to make the book as inclusive as possible. It is important to keep the claims of elitism and those of populism in some sort of balance. Poetry was never meant to be the handmaiden of politics or to have its values dictated by politicians. Harm can come from well-meaning efforts to turn poetry into an instrument for social change. But we should also bear in mind Walt Whitman's declaration that "the United States is the greatest poem."

A. R. ("Archie") Ammons, who made the selections for *The Best American Poetry 1994*, is one of America's best-loved poets. He has always been a maverick, and his long poems *Tape for the Turn of the Year* in the 1960s, *Sphere* and *The Snow Poems* in the 1970s, and *Garbage*, which was published in 1993, are extraordinary for their ambition, sweep, and inclusiveness. They are highly innovative without making a fetish of innovation as a value. And they are accompanied by a large body of shorter poems notable for their lyric intensity. For his works, Mr. Ammons has won a whole shelf of poetry prizes, fellowships, and awards. Archie and I are longtime neighbors in Ithaca, New York, and we talk about poetry regularly and often, so the work on this anthology was as if continuous with a conversation that began many years ago. Readers will discover in *The Best American Poetry 1994* a wealth of long poems, including a controversial verse play. There is a sestina, a phantom elegy, a sequence of "cinematic" prose poems and one of "unholy" sonnets.

The remarkable frankness with which American poets, both male and female, write about sex and romance is reflected here. Other subjects that provoke our poets include baseball, death, science, nature, alcoholism, AIDS, childbirth, snow, the human anatomy, Greek mythology, Leni Riefenstahl, and John Cage. A year ago *Harper's* put *The Best American Poetry* on its Index, revealing that "the number of poems that rhyme" in the 1993 edition was "one." I trust this rhymewatch will be a regular feature in the magazine.

For me, an attraction of the series is the sense that we are making a record of the taste of our leading poets. (John Ashbery did the choosing for the inaugural volume, followed by Donald Hall, Jorie Graham, Mark Strand, Charles Simic, Louise Glück, and this year Mr. Ammons.) And there is a second critical function that the anthology performs, since each of the seventy-five poets represented in the book is encouraged to write a comment on the chosen poem. (Some decline—three poets represented in the 1993 edition of *The Best American Poetry* even used their space to denounce the idea—but most are happy to oblige.) Readers seem to like this feature a good deal, as do students in writing workshops; the disclosures tend to be less academic, and are almost always more revealing, than the stuff you get in the quarterlies. The prose of articulate poets is a delight.

But in the end there is no substitute for real honest-to-goodness criticism—criticism without fear or favor—preferably written by people who are not themselves poets. It is highly possible that the perennial crisis in poetry is really a crisis in the criticism of poetry. The poems in America are as various and as fresh and as new as they ever were in the land of dreams. It is indeed likely that someday someone will look back on our much maligned era and pronounce it a golden age for American poetry. People will say: Ashbery was in his prime, and Ammons, and Merrill, and Merwin, and Strand, and Glück, and Rich, and Wilbur, and . . . a dozen other names. It is a pity that the professors responsible for responding to the poems have largely abandoned the field, preferring the ethereal realms of literary theory: deconstruction in the 1980s, the New Historicism now. But perhaps the English department is the wrong place to look for the sort of vigorous, generous, spirited criticism that a healthy art form needs. It could be that a better hope lies with independent scholars, scholars without an academic affiliation: a noble category that has emerged in the last decade. And perhaps we should be expecting more from high school teachers, that vast underrated army, who have traditionally inspired young people with the lifelong love of poetry.

Given the natural enmity that is supposed to govern relations between the poet as a type and the critic as a type, it is awkward for me as a poet to stand up and say, "We need better critics"—it's a bit like an old-line liberal standing up and saying, "We need better conservatives." But the facts point to this conclusion. Until and unless there are critics to help educate the taste of our readership, separating the good from the bad, and propounding the principles of aesthetic judgment, we will run the risk of expanding that readership at the expense of the art itself. In the meanwhile we may take solace in the way the art has been flourishing, against the odds, and in defiance of the gloom-sayers. We may rejoice in the abundances of our common poetic heritage and try to add our own indelible contributions.

A. R. ("Archie") Ammons was born in Whiteville, North Carolina, in 1926. He grew up on a North Carolina farm during the Great Depression and started writing poetry aboard a U.S. Navy destroyer escort in the South Pacific. After studying science at Wake Forest University, he completed his education at Berkeley. He worked briefly as the principal of an elementary school in Cape Hatteras and later managed a biological glass factory in southern New Jersey. Since 1964 he has taught at Cornell University, where he is the Goldwin Smith Professor of Poetry. He was awarded a MacArthur Fellowship in 1981, the year the "genius awards" were introduced. He has also received the Bollingen Prize (for *Sphere*, in 1975), the National Book Critics Circle Award (for *A Coast of Trees*, in 1981), and the National Book Award, twice—for *Collected Poems: 1951–1971* in 1973 and for the book-length poem *Garbage* in 1993. All these titles were published by Norton. Ammons's other books include *Ommateum* (1955), *Tape for the Turn of the Year* (1965), *The Snow Poems* (1977), *Worldly Hopes* (1982), and *The Really Short Poems of A. R. Ammons* (1990). He and his wife live in Ithaca, New York.

INTRODUCTION

by A. R. Ammons

◇ ◇ ◇

Language is the medium that carries the inscription, but what is inscribed in poetry is action, not language. The body of the ice-skater is only the means to an inscription on ice. Beautiful as the body may be, the inscription does not exist for the purpose of the body but of what the body does, what its doings symbolize.

Magnificently great about poetry is that its action is like other actions. It stands not as an isolated, esoteric activity but as a formal and substantive essentializing of all action. The ice-skater cuts formal figures in which the precision of execution is a high value, or she emerges clownish on the ice and imitates the hilarious sloppy falls we all sometimes commit; the invention of free style is always instantaneous, however many years of practice are in evidence. She engages the tensions we seek that relate our moments to our stories; though she is at any given second only *there*, she writes in our minds the full disclosure of the action which we afterwards, perhaps ever after, contemplate as a source and model of what dynamics might be and what values they might emphasize.

So poetry for me is a symbolic action shown by language and revealing what we would have our behavior imitate or strive for. This is perhaps least of all to imply good behavior. It is often, as in ice-skating contests, a drive toward competition, dominance, and victory over others. It can be ruthless, as ruthless in its perhaps deceptive and small way as a Caesar or Khan in his great way.

Poets of unconventional appearance and behavior are in some periods greatly exposed to danger. An unconventional sexual proclivity, for example, can induce hatred to the point of murder. To thrive in such a world, the poet must disguise himself so as to live efficiently enough with others to risk revealing himself. Insects' bodies imitate twigs and leaves so as to be present but invisible to their predators. When they are most visible, flashing bright oranges and reds, their gambit is to advertise openly that they are poisonous if eaten. Poets are sometimes glaringly unconventional and so are openly ostracized, but even the hostile enforcers of social codes may want, half-willingly, to be free, as free as the artist they profess to despise. Poets deceive to protect themselves; they may need to transform their strategies before they take the sometimes heavy chance of bringing forward a work of true originality. History is full of this, of this most of all.

Poetry is not innocent, not sweet, not just sweet. It charms to convince, deceive, make room, find a way to autonomy and freedom. We owe to those who deal at the center of these dynamics the vitality of our lives.

In recent years literary criticism has greatly enriched itself by strong solicitations of the poem. I suppose we should all be grateful for the critical positionings that have permitted us to look anew at our fundamental estimates of what poems are or can be. I think no one would choose to go on indefinitely with unalterable programs touching our use of words. Even if we ultimately settle for a slight change of perspective when we had at first supposed a revolution of values was upon us, we are likely to be grateful for both the initial pleasant disturbance and the bit of freshness detectable in the aftermath.

So I for one—and this is one time I assume majorities agree with me—am delighted with the stir that has lately surrounded the art, especially the literary art, scene. My knowledge of the origin and nature of recent theoretical investigation has arrived not by patient study on my part (I am a totalized student of incidentals, pop-ups, and other adventitiousnesses) but by whiffs of intimation already in their fifth or sixth remove from virtual communication or reception. But I am still delighted, however amateurishly, because so much of the philosophical or critical discourse has had at its center— guess what?—poems, and since I never expected secondary elaboration or clever stance to do away with what I feel to be alive at the center of poems (even, sometimes, in their peripheries, and even when the peripheries spread out until there seems little if any relation between one iota and another: not to go on too far with the figure, I mean, for example, as stars on the outrims of galaxies nearly lose their orientations with the core), I am peculiarly, perhaps, without complaint.

I think the thing that got me was when the critics began to encourage the view of themselves as no longer subject to or dependent on poems but in a higher register of influx than poets or poems. I found this particularly amusing because the critics, having all tried to write poems themselves, had apparently turned to criticism in order to have reason to pursue literature, a clean and noble calling in which even the grubbing is fairly clean and, in many cases, financially rewarding. I read the poems I could find by the critics, and I pronounced them not very good. I wondered then just what it is about critics that enables them to know so much about poetry when they obviously don't have the faintest idea how it comes about.

But I concluded I was just having a foolish fuss with myself. There is no reason ever in the world for the critic and poet to be at odds, and for the following reason: the primary motion of the poet is to put things together and touch a source that feels like life—at times even more powerful than life. It is a synthesis of analogies and associations that promotes, in the best hands, and even when disjunctive, a sense of renewed vitality. That is what one feels. That is a fact whether noticed by poet or critic. The critic makes another kind of synthesis; his or her synthesis comes as a result of what can be added up after taking things apart. What is added up, as in dissertations and works of critical discourse, is thought to be subtler and finer than the work that gave rise to it. But that cannot be, because the two modes of thought, the creative and the analytical, are not comparable; they are apples and oranges.

I could go on with this at great length and probably even convince you, if you aren't convinced already, that I am right, but my purpose moves beyond such prideful discriminations.

I am just afraid that young poets have not known how to resist the incursions and mock conquests except by the usual gift of paying no attention to them. I think poets should strive to be ready to counter assaults in any language whatever, and I will try to give you mine, simple and humble as it is.

When exposition has allowed the poem to arrive, its sentences, rhythms, figures coming together or one after the other, the poem ends. At that point, the exposition ceases and the poem stands whole, a disposition of parts, of movement laid out finished and still, like an object. Suppose the object now to be a stone you pick up beside the road and bring to class: you place the stone on the seminar table and ask your students to write about it. Its history can be discussed in terms of the shape its dissolution has taken. A sample can be taken from it for analysis. Its age can be determined. Chronology may be determinable in its layering. In other words, numberless papers, including chemical and atomic notations, can be written, but the stone, apart from its missing specimen, is unaffected. The writings about the stone do not replace the stone. Nothing can replace the stone. It is itself in its own integrity or shambles.

Poems are like that. They come on in a sound stream that cannot be talked away, and any other way of representing the sound stream will not be the same sound stream. Poems to the extent that they are dispositions, not expositions, are nonverbal, just like a stone or a piece of sculpture. Thousands of papers can be written about Rodin and many of them may know more about Rodin than Rodin did but they will not resemble sculpture. Rodin made the sculptures. No one else did.

Until they end, poems exist in time from the first syllable to the last. They are actions. Emerson said that words are a kind of action. Aristotle called drama an imitation of life. Verbal actions imitate human actions or the actions of wind or river or rain. Poems are actions, of which one action is the making of statements. People behave and as a part of that behavior they express opinions, observations, assertions. But the assertion can be the opposite of what the behavior means. If on a January day in upstate New York a person perhaps given to light humor says, "A boiler, isn't it?," you know it's cold outside.

I'm trying not to go on at too great length, but at the same time I risk losing your attention if I don't give you the means to follow me. I say that the behavior of a poem, good or bad behavior, gives us access to a knowledge of the meaning of behavior in our time. For example, a heroic couplet, reasoned and rhymed, is *characteristic* of a certain style of mind and action that identifies a period. A short poem, pure to the exclusion of every challenge, is one style of life. A sprawling, inclusive poem tells us what it is in addition to what it says or says it is.

Value is represented in poems. Poems exemplify ways to behave. We can write poems that disintegrate before the reader's eyes, and by that we can mean that we refuse to respect the values of our day. The poem can be accessible or distraught, harsh or melodic, abstract or graphic, and from these traits we can form our own models and traits.

The question I ask of a poem is: What way of life does this poem seem to be representing? Is it light, witty, lugubrious, generous, mean-spirited? How does it behave? Should I behave that way? If poems are still capable of so strong a communication, however impressionistically derived, am I to think that poetry has become decentered "texts" first of all? Am I to suppose that a sloppy artist is not perhaps advocating sloppiness as a way of life, and isn't it possible that the meticulous poem can be the more beautifully finished the more disgusting? Hasn't behavior perceived early on as bad become the very image of a later good?

Poetry's actions are like other actions. They are at once actions themselves and symbolic actions, representative models of behavior. As long as I have the feeling that poems are capable of evidencing matters of such crucial importance, I will not think that much has changed: poems come from where they always came from; they dance in themselves as they always have; they sing to us as they always will, and we will not need to be told what we feel or which way our inclinations lean, or what there is new and lean to find in them. We will dance and sing. Sometime later we will *talk about* singing and dancing, and in that effort, we will need all the help we can get from the critics or anyone else.

THE
BEST
AMERICAN
POETRY
1994

◇　◇　◇

DICK ALLEN

A Short History of the Vietnam War Years

◊ ◊ ◊

Nothing was said until the house grew dark
And a fishnet of stars was cast upon its windows.
In the tall bedroom mirror, the door to Watergate
Opened again. A helicopter tiny as a moth
Flew across the lovers' flanks, its slow pinwheel blades
Making the sound of grief and churning rivers.

Placards lifted, the marchers of the Sixties
Stood in green meadows. Then folk songs began
Rising from their lips like blue leaves in summer
And time was a slipstream where a Phantom jet
Rolled in the sun. The lovers ran their hands
Over the rice fields and the panting oxen.

Deep in itself, the bedside clock unwound
By the edge of a pool, casting its minutes out
To a shoal of Destroyers. *Be still*, the lovers whispered.
In the room above the hall a mud-stained jeep
Backed up to a wooden brothel in Saigon,
An orange-robed monk knelt down in billowed flame.

The lovers grew sad. A soft rainy wind from Ohio
Brushed gunfire bursts and tear gas over them.
We will never love money, they said, clinging to each other,
Or dress like television, work like I.B.M.
We will grow flowers to slide into rifle barrels,
And we will dance barefoot on Wall Street's glass chin.

That was when hope was a temple bell, a bleeding eye,
A circle of books around the lovers' bed
As the soldiers looked on. Mai Lai fell half-asleep
Under the full thrust moon. On bruised hands and knees,
Tet advanced along the shadowed railroad ties
And the deltas awoke and flooded Washington.

We will drift to Cambodia, the lovers said,
Dance in People's Park, burn incense tapers
At Buddhist shrines. The house wrapped its black armband
Over the lovers as they lay entwined.
And if you listened, you could hear the mortar fire
Walking up the valleys like an old blind man.

from *The Gettysburg Review*

TOM ANDREWS

Cinema Vérité

◊   ◊   ◊

CINEMA VÉRITÉ: THE DEATH OF ALFRED, LORD TENNYSON

The camera pans a gorgeous snow-filled landscape: rolling hills, large black trees, a frozen river. The snow falls and falls. The camera stops to find Tennyson, in an armchair, in the middle of a snowy field.

Tennyson:
It's snowing. The snow is like . . . the snow is like crushed
   aspirin,
like bits of paper . . . no, it's like gauze bandages, clean
   teeth, shoelaces, headlights . . . no,
I'm getting too old for this, it's like a huge T-shirt
   that's been chewed on by a dog,
it's like semen, confetti, chalk, sea shells, woodsmoke,
   ash, soap, trillium, solitude, daydreaming . . . Oh hell,
you can see for yourself! That's what I hate about film!

He dies.

CINEMA VÉRITÉ: WILLIAM MAKEPEACE THACKERAY FOLLOWS HIS BLISS

The Fairfield County Fair in Lancaster, Ohio. Shots of Thackeray on the Ferris Wheel, the bumper cars, at the livestock auction, drinking beer at the demolition derby. Cut to Thackeray at the concession stand.

Thackeray: I can't make up my mind between Elephant Ears and a chili dog.

Concessionaire: Oh, go ahead, Mr. Thackeray, get both. You deserve it.

Thackeray: You're right. What the hell, Elephant Ears and chili dogs for everyone! They're on me!

Assembled passersby *(in chorus)*: Oh boy! Thank you, William Makepeace Thackeray, possessor of one of the strangest middle names in history!

The fair comes to a halt as Thackeray is lifted and carried through the streets of Lancaster . . .

CINEMA VÉRITÉ: JACQUES DERRIDA
AND GOD'S *TSIMTSUM*

An intensely exciting montage of Macchu Picchu, erupting volcanos, North Pole glaciers, cells multiplying, Brazilian rainforests, $E = MC^2$, 200 MeV, undersea vistas, the Milky Way, etc., eventually leading us to the Mount of Olives, where God and Derrida loaf, the latter holding a Camcorder.

God: I withdraw from Myself into Myself to provide a space and an occasion for all creation.

Derrida *(flustered, shaking the Camcorder)*: Wait a minute . . . Which button do I press? . . .

Videotape streams and spills out of the Camcorder . . .

from *Field*

JOHN ASHBERY

Myrtle

◊   ◊   ◊

How funny your name would be
if you could follow it back to where
the first person thought of saying it,
naming himself that, or maybe
some other persons thought of it
and named that person. It would
be like following a river to its source,
which would be impossible. Rivers have no source.
They just automatically appear at a place
where they get wider, and soon a real
river comes along, with fish and debris,
regal as you please, and someone
has already given it a name: St. Benno
(saints are popular for this purpose) or, or
some other name, the name of his
long-lost girlfriend, who comes
at long last to impersonate that river,
on a stage, her voice clanking
like its bed, her clothing of sand
and pasted paper, a piece of real technology,
while all along she is thinking, I can
do what I want to do. But I want to stay here.

from *The New Yorker*

Tremendous Mood Swings

◇　◇　◇

Clearly we'd found the rim of something.
No sooner were we skirting
its edges for the purpose of a clear outline,
than every step seemed possible

infraction; the inlet had frozen
and our excursions crazed
the surface; extreme cold, we're informed,
changes the properties of things:

the untraversable yields an effortless walk;
barriers fill with passages:
and we fill dimensions where others belong,
maintain stances of others'

walking, and suspect vaguely
"We do not belong here": this is nudity
stripped of liberation.
I'm not sure how we arrived at this point.

If the water makes a half-circle
in the land, wouldn't we observe where one stops?
"The perimeter's a foregone conclusion."
Or so we thought, but as we traverse

this scene, certain that events will fall into
line, that already we sense the emerging
figure, it seems the sturdiest thing we have
is to witness convictions erode and form

and frame us. So, is the question
"What does it look like here?" or
"What's holding us up?"
But there is more.

This presumably illegal recording.
I'm unclear who is playing
these different instruments.
The integrity of the sound changes

as a young man makes his way
around the room, microphones concealed
in his sleeves. One hears him as he attempts to
near the source of the sound;

his efforts, though, become vague
approximations; they do not originate
where he'd thought them:
this hum means the circulation of blood,

static means bodies have touched.
Then to interrupt the recording midperformance
and rebegin from that distance:
what authority or love he must have seen.

But one's left wishing the voice
could continue where it left off;
this interest in ghosts is humiliating, but it can't be stopped.
Wanting the event to continue before it ends,

like lovers so anxious for one another,
they become negligent and resentful.
This is how I hear it now: so wild for the sound,
he tries to bring it inside of him,

certain the sounds carry messages
he can't keep pace with.
It is everything I hear: interference and persistent
buzzing and I know I have lost you.

from *Grand Street*

CYNTHIA BOND

What You Want Means
What You Can Afford

◊   ◊   ◊

I'm sensitive to what the traffic will
allow to this convergence. If the
wrong way's wended we'll end it off
an off ramp slack cul-de-sac. And
see I've got bends beyond that belief;
I mean to jam it up to paralysis,
clip full seconds the take of a curve
and finagle a pass on the right just
past the last possible exit out the
respectable avenue. Needn't wonder
feckless, mapless; wander reckless
through a permanent, concrete
attachment. I'm talking here foundations
way long poured, civil stuff gone native
under long duress. I'm driving a literal
conversation.

from *Ascent*

Demographics

◊ ◊ ◊

They don't want to stop. They can't stop.
    They've been going at it for days now,
for hours, for months, for years. He's on top
    of her. She's on top of him. He's licking
her between the legs. Her fingers
    are in his mouth. It's November.
It's March. It's July and there are palms.
    Palms and humidity. It's the same man.
It's a different man. It's August and slabs
    of heat waves wallow on tarred lots.
Tornadoes sprawl across open plains.
    Temperatures rise. Rains accumulate.
Somewhere a thunderstorm dies. Somewhere
    a snow falls, colored by the red dust
of a desert. She spreads her legs. His lips
    suck her nipples. She smells his neck.
It's morning. It's night. It's noon.
    It's this year. It's last year. It's 4 a.m.
It started when the city shifted growth
    to the north, over the underground
water supply. Now the back roads are gone
    where they would drive, the deer glaring into
the headlights, Wetmore and Thousand Oaks,
    and the ranch roads that led to the hill country
and to a trio of deep moving rivers.
    There were low water crossings. Flood gauges.
Signs for falling rock. There were deer blinds
    for sale. There was cedar in the air.

Her hands are on his hips. He's pushing
   her up and down. There are so many things
she's forgotten. The names of trees. Wars.
   Recipes. The trench graves filled with hundreds.
Was it Bolivia? Argentina? Chile?
   Was it white gladioli that decorated the altar
where wedding vows were said? There was
   a dance floor. Tejano classics.
A motel. A shattered mirror. Flies.
   A Sunbelt sixteen wheeler. Dairy Queens.
Gas stations. The smell of piss and cement.
   There was a field of corn, or was it cotton?
There were yellow trains and silver silos.
   They can't stop. They don't want to stop.
It's Spring, and five billion inhale
   and exhale across two hemispheres. Oceans
form currents and counter-currents.
   There was grassland. There was sugar cane.
There were oxen. Metallic ores.
   There was Timber. Fur-bearing animals.
Rice lands. Industry. Tundra. Winds
   cool the earth's surface. Thighs press
against thighs. Levels of water fluctuate.
   And yesterday a lightning bolt reached
a temperature hotter than the sun.

from *TriQuarterly*

The Fire Fetched Down

◇　◇　◇

When they knew what he had given them,
This florid colossus with the sunrise in his eyes
And skin the color of perfectly ripened fruit,
Understood what he had done in the name of freedom,
Of self-esteem, their first thought was to give it back,
Who had been happy in their miserable condition,
Had been content each hour to kill or cringe,
Pleased to end their days in the detached mercy
Of stupent sense, the sweet shock that flesh is air to;
When they saw what he intended, this monstrous
Avatar wrapped in conceits of agony, of honor,
Their every instinct (before such brute reflex
Was blunted by the dull weight of the abstract)
Was to spurn the bounty, slay the bearer, to destroy
The visiting light, its unwanted complication.
After all, his differences had not been theirs,
His absurd dispute with the divine, his squabble
About a sacred ox and some celestial secret;
His ambition for their state was nothing they could grasp,
And they wished only to be as they had been, dying
To extinguish the moted mazy rays that floated
Like gleaming locks on his titanic head, to blot out
The subtle moonbeams that shone so as he smiled. . . .
But the fire he brought was beautiful, a jewel
Of countless facets, a spectrum infinitely broad,
An aethereal motion they never tired of looking on;
The flame was gorgeous, and they were human,

And they took that gift, reaching to accept
The ember of ideas, the conflagration of tongues,
And then his name was their name (*Forethought,
Premonition*, how the word had frightened them!),
And his pain became theirs, too,
Chained in the rational abyss and torn
Time and again by cruel and busy claws, raked
By the razor bill of what they could conclude.

from *The Paris Review*

me against the world

◇ ◇ ◇

when I was a kid
one of the questions asked was,
would you rather eat a bucket of shit
or drink a bucket of piss?
I thought that was easy.
"that's easy," I said, "I'll take the
piss."
"maybe we'll make you do both,"
they told me.
I was the new kid in the
neighborhood.
"oh yeah," I said.
"yeah!" they said.
there were 4 of them.
"yeah," I said, "you and whose
army?"
"we won't need no army," the
biggest one said.
I slammed my fist into his
stomach.
then all 5 of us were down on
the ground fighting.
they got in each other's way
but there were still too many
of them.
I broke free and started
running.
"sissy! sissy!" they yelled.
"going home to mama?"

I kept running.
they were right.
I ran all the way to my house,
up the driveway and onto the
porch and into the
house
where my father was beating
up my mother.
she was screaming.
things were broken on the floor.
I charged my father and started swinging.
I reached up but he was too tall,
all I could hit were his
legs.
then there was a flash of red and
purple and green
and I was on the floor.
"you little prick!" my father said,
"you stay out of this!"
"don't you hit my boy!" my mother
screamed.
but I felt good because my father
was no longer hitting my
mother.
to make sure, I got up and charged
him again, swinging.
there was another flash of colors
and I was on the floor
again.
when I got up again
my father was sitting in one chair
and my mother was sitting in
another chair
and they both just sat there
looking at me.
I walked down the hall and into
my bedroom and sat on the
bed.
I listened to make sure there
weren't any more sounds of

beating and screaming
out there.
there weren't.
then I didn't know what to
do.
it wasn't any good outside
and it wasn't any good
inside.
so I just sat there.
then I saw a spider making a web
across a window.
I found a match, walked over,
lit it and burned the spider to
death.
then I felt better.
much better.

from *Urbanus*

The Only Dance There Is

◊   ◊   ◊

Oh no! He's going to *show* it to me—
This gelatinous spore burst like a shot bird's foot—
Splayed, in the nest of his own little egg cup ear. God!
Is it he, or is it I, in my white spikes and Levi's,
Peeling sweaty red labels off Buds, who becomes
Slowly exposed, a pornographic snap developing
At a While-U-Wate Shak? Is it my turquoise lighter holder,
Or my voice, full of coins and strangulations,
That compels the alcoholics, the men I literally live for,
To repeatedly ask what I want? "Hey! What do you want?"
I know girls who dance in bars and marry, like, firemen.
This man here is so unemployed I could talk to him
All night. I'm saddled on a teetering labrador of lust, drunk
And ready to fill up a station wagon. It is

         the *degringolade* of the species of woman I am—
The curl of my big leg and the sure smell of that sweat,
Redolent and in that Terrible Vicinity. Here, *let me buy that*,
I am transmigrating in the *def leppard* of my "desire"
And it has happened before, is happening, will happen again,
All of it. It's the old lovemaking in the cemetery routine, Johnny.
The last beauty I fell for drank me AND fucked me
Under the table. He said, "Hey there, you little redheaded
         sweetiepie, you.
Perfection, my life is an open casket funeral; darling,
Our love is the visitation hour." You heard what he did next.
Frankly I still admire him.
I have nevernever touched myself so well,
Nor could I observe a man jerk off in a sock with such joy.

At times I swear the sex of the earth is a bedwash and sponge for
         Jesus.
At times I swear I could live with a man I'll call "Tom"

         forever: when we met he bound me with Venetian blind cord
And went down on me for roughly nine hours. He delivered
His own daughters' sons. You know how it must be for me.
Drunk in bars, I feel the righteous *ness* of humidity and cherry,
Initials carved in tequila-drenched grain with "surgical precision."
We are listing toward the primordial wind and I talk about men
To men. (Once, my hair caught fire in a tavern.
         The man who set it horsewhipped my head, singeing
         His shavebrush Stetson.)
An absolute glance. Tufts of a botched permanent wave. O,
You drunk and fucked-up munificence. O, Unshaven, Midnight,
Kindly lubricate my introduction to your unspeakable ring of chaos
You understand to be your life. You will surely pull the coil out of
         my car.
Oh no! He's going to show it to me—
God save the two of us, supernova.

         from *New England Review*

A Catalpa Tree on West Twelfth Street

◇ ◇ ◇

While the sun stops, or
seems to, to define a term
for the interminable,
the human aspect, here
in the West Village, spindles
to a mutilated dazzle—

niched shards of solitude
embedded in these brownstone
walkups such that the Hudson
at the foot of Twelfth Street
might be a thing that's
done with mirrors: definition

by deracination—grunge,
hip-hop, Chinese takeout,
co-ops—while the globe's
elixir caters, year by year,
to the resurgence of this
climbing tentpole, frilled and stippled

yet again with bloom
to greet the solstice:
What year was it it over-

took the fire escape? The
roof's its next objective.
Will posterity (if there

is any) pause to regret
such layerings of shade,
their cadenced crests' trans-
valuation of decay, the dust
and perfume of an all
too terminable process?

from *The New York Times*

Tantrum Girl Responds to Death

◊ ◊ ◊

COOKIE

cookie was hard the way only women can be hard/ not street or
drug tough but more like that roughness certain women steal/
thieves of male power/ shirts & short hair cuts/ pull up boots/
like a steel rod suspended through the shoulders/ w/ musculature
molded from the men's camp/ & a stride w/ all the power of a
honest erection/ but w/out the greed

MY THING

i keep my hair long for lesbian get togethers/ i always wear skirts
& bangles/ my wish is for the mannish type to wish their yin into
my yang/ cookie had serious flirt going on/ not nobody for no deep
conversation/ not my type for the steady thing/ cookie: you ain't
nobody to talk to so why trip because you died

CANCER

from lumps of stress lodged in her breasts/ shrunk in a hospital
room while chicken shit members of her family shunned their bull
dagger daughter/ son wouldn't call/ & all the queer christians took
turns driving out to cucamonga/ gay people death vigil & the hot
wire phone tree w/ news of her weight loss/ cookie, big chested,
greedy eater at our card parties, shriveled down to bones & a non-
sense daze sinking in her eyesockets

KADDISH

it's happening/ it's happening/ like a virus of the boys got confused
& stole a body in our camp/ it's happening that fat cookie is dying/
big, lusty, bull dyke cookie is coming down/ breaking down/ mak-
ing ruins of her body/ the dark of her eyes detach/ the needles &
tubes sound ugly mantras & stink/ all spirit crushed by collapsing
organs/ all soul silent/ & traceless

SO WHAT

she didn't know me/ i winked at her/ i dragged her into my mastur-
bation fantasies/ i tried to lift my skirt & wave the vanilla scent i
use to lure butch gay girls/ sex & death is dancing/ death who can't
get me like mothers & folks w/ functional families/ death who lets
me know when i'm in love/ fear of death who leaves me when i'm
bored/ when i'm arrogant

FUNERAL HOME

a cave of refrigeration/ the chest of the undertaker sunk in the
center/ his eyes have no history/ his mouth no natural heat/ num-
bers in his mind like i get off at 7/ it's tuesday/ twelfth funeral this
week/ thirty two hundred dollars/ room #5/ services at 8/ caskets
in cells w/ low ceilings/ cells w/ sticky dust

VISION

i am on guard for perversion/ i am hunting the lessons of death/ i
seek strange details/ the discharge left in the hollows of a rotten
life/ the excrements of love liars/ i'm sorry i never got her in bed/
i don't give a care except to watch you/ death presses at my temples/
i am ready to rebel/ i will never have children/ i shiver like death
needs a tantrum/ a cheerleader/ a lesbian lover screamer girl

PEARLS

cookie has on pearls w/ rosy rouge/ cookie has puffed out hair &
bad taste secretary's bow tie/ cookie looks like somebody's auntie,
who had parakeets & ate biscuits/ they manicured her nails & hung

white plastic jewelry from her ears/ her body a complex lie of femininity/ the closet of a casket/ her pearls the polished bones of fish enslaved by men

DEAD MEETING OF THE FAMILY

all her blood relatives dressed in black & shine/ marched in from the void they left in the cancer ward & took up the front rows of the home/ her son who called her freakish/ her nana who cursed her sinful mouth/ her mom who beat her through her boyish adolescence/ gripped hands & slung snot/ wailing for cookie to pass into the peace of the male god/ faggots & lesbians who saw death empty her face/ cornered/ crowded in the row in the back

VISION EXPLOSION

i talk to my fingers/ touch her, i say/ this is your chance/ will she feel like furniture/ death in the flesh w/ no real reason to mourn/ & sorrow ropes my throat/ you ain't no femme, i tell cookie/ you wasn't no frustrated straight girl i scream/ you was a natural bulldagger/ a lesbian ass woman/ i ain't lying just cause you dead/ cause your momma wanna front the betrayal off/ & by then they are on to me/ & they pull me back into line

TANTRUM GIRL RESPONDS TO DEATH

i swallow the lesson like pills from a wealthy doctor/ i ingest the family tribute like more proof against blood bonding/ & i calm down off the death addiction/ just in case death has a parasite clause/ don't wanna this shit sticking to me/ don't wanna pay for arrogance in the death of some beloved/ death could come around & kick my ass good/

from *The Kenyon Review*

Sestina

◇ ◇ ◇

So bondage is a big part of it, after all—
that old art of rendering a lover submissive:
a tactic, a strategy. Denying somebody's body
the power to move denies that body the power
to be believed. Isn't that what's so sexual?
The intimate plea? The fear you can't go back?

Until your lover throws you over on your back.
Maybe a woman becomes a man, then. After all,
it's the head games that conjure up the sexual:
which one agrees, this time, to be submissive;
which one straps on the fetishes, the powers,
we make to make the body yield up the body . . .

O the rendering, the surrendering of the body!
We so much want to go back, all the way back . . .
You stand before a mirror, naked, the power
of someone's eyes, words, erasing you, the all
you claim to be. Belief can be so submissive:
desire, not truth. But being believed is sexual

vantage: the crying out, the echo, the sexual
need you never knew could subjugate the body . . .
So you cry out at the idea of her, submissive,
yes, her hands your hands, *yes,* leading you back,
her voice your voice, *o god,* eyes lips cunt all
mirroring, *yes,* the glory, *o god yes,* the power . . .

Later, you wipe off the remnants of the power
with Kleenex. When you get down to the sexual
level, you get sexually levelled, that's all:
doesn't discipline make a believer of the body?
You whisper no name but hers in the going back.
Tomorrow, it will be her turn to be submissive:

the ties that bind render you both submissive.
You'll need her to believe your plea, her power;
she'll need you to escort her all the way back,
before the life alongside this life, her body
alongside yours: ravenous, indifferent, sexual.
There, anything might happen, anything at all,

if all you need is to be believed. The power
of the sexual plea masquerades as the submissive
act. The body is the flower of the going back.

from *The Paris Review*

full of rain, the word

◊ ◊ ◊

full of rain, the word
is coming now
out of the south, out of
                the flat white grain
                of rice that sleeps
still inside the husk, in Bellary, that waits
            for a woman's hand,
            for the winnowing
and whisper
of fallen stalk, the word

is coming now
out of the north, out of
                the faint, the murmuring
                sounds the stone
                makes to itself
as it watches the clothes
beaten on its crude
                and eaten back
                at the Krishna
and the Godavari.

                out of the wooden plough
                dragged out of the east
across the hardened field
by buffalo, in Bengal, Orissa,
            out of the west
            by cows stretched thin

around the ribs, in Gujarat, Maharashtra
out of the tin
        the village beggar holds,
        out of her eyes
grown heavy and dull,
dull with the heavy
        abrasion of desire, out of

the mud the buffaloes
wallow in, out of the mud
        that builds the hut and breaks

in flood, out of
the weeping mud. The word,
        it sleeps like a fallen god
        in the flat dung-
cakes the women smear
on brick walls, washed

                white with lime, it
                burns

in that burning of dung,
open fires and wood
        spelling smoke in thick
        letters in the air, the word
rushes at us with the whole
alphabet
        of the monsoon
        in its wake—

but such a distanced
whisper, such a shaved,
whittled breath,
                who will hear
                the word as it struggles,
                who will put

their ear to the stones and to
the grain snapped hard
off the singing stalk, who will
        touch the swollen
        word and know
        what it says, who will hear
        the voice of the poor
        as they speak?

from *Green Mountains Review*

THOMAS M. DISCH

The Cardinal Detoxes:
A Play in One Act

◇ ◇ ◇

*We are a sinful church. We are naked. Our anger,
our pain, our anguish, our shame, are clear to the
whole world.*
—The Most Reverend Alphonsus L. Penney,
D.D., Archbishop of St. John's,
Newfoundland, in his statement of
resignation July 18, 1990

*The scene is a monastically bare cell in a Catholic detox center run by the
Brothers of the Most Holy Blood. There is a bed, a small night table beside
it, a desk and chair, and a prie-dieu. On the wall above the bed, a crucifix,
flanked by pictures of the Sacred Heart and Mater Dolorosa.*

*The Cardinal and a Brother of the Most Holy Blood are discovered as the
lights come up. The Cardinal in a state of nerves; the Brother stands by
the door, attentive but inexpressive, except at rare moments when the
Cardinal has said something particularly offensive to conventional piety or
pious convention. After any action he has been called to perform, the
Brother returns to his post of duty before the door.*

THE CARDINAL:

God. For the most part I do without
Him. Don't we all. He leaves us no choice,
Having left us, bereft us, at some point

In pre-history—say, at the moment Christ
Particularly complained of. Was that before
Or after the gall was proffered him? Say what?
Oh, yes, I know, it is your vow to say
Nothing at all. The merest sponge for all
My vinegar. And speaking of vinegar . . . ?

*The Brother nods, leaves the room a moment and returns with a bottle of
white wine and a wineglass on a tray. He places this on the night table,
fills the glass half-full, and gives it to the Cardinal, who takes a sip and
makes a sour face.*

THE CARDINAL:

Where do you find this wine? The tears of Christ,
Indeed! He would have died before he drank
This piss. But piss is sacred, too, if it
Is His, and I consume it reverently,
Having—had you supposed?—whispered the words,
The abracadabra, of consecration.
What priest, what Catholic, does not imagine
Every drop as somehow holy? Dregs
Of the wedding feast, lees of the Last Supper: this
Is my blood—
                        [*sips*]
                —or soon enough will be.
It is kind of the Abbot to accommodate
My evening need to transubstantiate.
He doubtless sees it as the loosener of
My tongue. Is the recorder on? I know
I'm being bugged, but that's all one to me.
So long as you employ corkscrews and not
Thumbscrews, I will unfold my heresies
With all due pomp, a true heresiarch.
But the Abbot ought to know I'm not
The sort of heretic the Church is prone
To burn. In matters that concern the Faith
I am as orthodox as any pope.
The Trinity, the Virgin Birth, the fall

Of Adam and the fault of Eve,
The fleshy Resurrection of the Dead,
Whatever's set down in the Creed, or been
Decreed by any Vicar of the Church—
In all this I have Faith. What I believe's
Another thing. Belief's involuntary;
Faith's an act of will, more powerful
As it demands credence in what we can't
Believe. Were I the Pope, I'd elevate
The Shroud of Turin to an article
Of faith; I would declare the round world flat
And build basilicas on Ararat.
So much for Faith; in morals, as well, I am
Ultra-montane. Priestly celibacy?
I agree. No contraception but
By abstinence. No sodomy. You look
Askance? Surely we must seal the back door,
If we lock up the front. Carnality will out,
No doubt, even among our holy few,
But all in cloistered silence, stealthily.
AIDS, alas, has made it hard to keep
Our sepulchres properly spotless. Even
Among you Brothers of the Holy Blood,
I hear, there have been actuarial
Anomalies. One abbot dead, another
Ailing, or so it's said. Well, there have been
Plagues before, and there'll be plagues again.
Please don't suppose I'm being holier
Than thou and thine. Would I be serving time
In detox if I hadn't erred as well?

He sits down on the bed and looks to the Brother for a glance of permission,
then pours another glass of wine.

THE CARDINAL:

I *do* repent me of the woman's death:
Mother of four and pregnant with a fifth;
A Catholic to boot. Had I had doubts

Of God's ambition as a dramatist,
They'd be resolved with this: CARDINAL FLYNN,
INTOXICATED, REAR-ENDS PREGNANT MOM—
They're always "Moms" in newspapers—a Mom,
What's more, who was my own parishioner.
It is deplorable, and I deplore it.
Do I, as well, blame God? Who iced the road
And sent her Chevy somersaulting? No.
I doubt that God's as meddlesome as that.
Newton's laws of motion did the job
Without His intervention. God, if He's
Not dead, is deaf, indifferent, or asleep.
For me, for most of us, God is a sham—
An ancient Poetry: I Am That I Am,
As who is not? I'm what I am, too—a priest,
A whited sepulchre, a drunken beast—
According to the *Times-Despatch* and *Sun*—
A criminal, though yet, with any luck,
The diocese will pay whatever price
The prosecution asks to drop the charge.
It wouldn't do, would it, to have My Grace
Be sent away, however many drinks
I may have had. Archbishops are not put
In jail. I wonder what they *will* have done
With me. You wouldn't know? Or wouldn't say.
Yours is the vow *I* ought to take—Silence!
But silence never was my forte. My forte
Is speech, and I will use it if I must.
I trust the tape recorder is still on?
Then this is what I mean to do, the same
As any minor mafioso caught
And facing time: I'll sing. I'll tell those things
We Cardinals and Archbishops say
Among ourselves, the secret wisdom of
The Church, its policies and stratagems,
Beginning with the obvious. Just guess.

He pours more wine, savoring the Brother's baleful looks.

THE CARDINAL:

Abortion, naturally. It is the cause
To knit our ever fewer faithful few
By giving them an enemy to fight,
Those murderous liberal bitches who refuse
To be a Mom. It is the wolf who herds
The sheep; the shepherd but assists, and sheep
Know this. Wolfless, they'll stray beyond the reach
Of hook and crook. Just look at the mess we're in.
No one attends Mass but the senile poor.
Detroit has simply given up the ghost
And closed its churches as the surest way
To staunch the flow of cash. Even where there
Is money, Faith's extinct—and Brotherhood,
The kind that's formed by cotes and ghetto walls.
Consider Poland, Northern Ireland,
Or *my* Archdiocese before this age
Of wishy-washy tolerance, when we
Were wops and micks and spics and krauts and built
The churches that stand empty now. The WASP
Majority was our oppressor then,
But now? Who hates us? Whom have we to fear?
Jews served the purpose for a while, and still
One meets the odd parishioner who feels
A pang of loss for Father Coughlin. Glemp,
In Poland, still baits Jews—the five or six
Surviving there. But after Auschwitz, how
Shall Holy Mother Church pursue that course?
The Jews, in any case, are not our problem:
Our problem's women. Ah-ha! Your eyes agree.
It's something every cleric understands.
It's what we mean by harping on the theme
Of family values and the sanctity
Of life, i.e., a way of bringing up
Men to be men, women to be slaves,
And priests to be their overseers. Think
Of Italy. For centuries the Church
Beneficently engineered the codes
Of gender so each Giacomo would have

His Jill, his family fiefdom, and his fill
Of sex, or if not quite his fill, his bare
Sufficiency, while she, the Mom, kept dumb
Or mumbled rosaries. Beyond the pale
Of family, the convent and the brothel
Took up the overflow of those who balked
At their Madonnament. The benefit
To all men of sufficient strength of mind
Should be self-evident; the rest could join
The Church, and practice harsh austerities
Expressive of a holy impotence,
Or else become the system's managers.
Of course, it's not just Italy of which
I speak: it's you and me. It's Fatherhood
In all the Mother Church's Fatherlands.
And it's *women* who've rebelled, thrown off
The yoke of meek subservience becoming
Handmaids of the Lord Their Spouse, who would address
The Angel of Annunciation: "No,
I've better things to do just now than bear
A child. When I am ready, *I'll* tell you."
Women demand equality, and no one
Has been able to gainsay them. They have
The vote, the pill, the freedom of the street.
Now they'd be priests! They do not understand
When they have won their last demand, there'll be
No Church but just Detroit writ large. For why
Should men go on pretending they believe
In all our Bulls, if somehow they don't stand
To benefit? They will walk out the door.
Not all of them and all at once, of course.
Some unisex parents for a while will rear
Mini-families of one or two,
As now the wealthier Protestants do.
What's to be done? Redraw the line again?
Admit the ladies and admit the Church
Was wrong? Declare the Fathers of the Church
This age's Ptolemys, ruled out-of-date
By schoolmarm Galileos? Rather turn
Our churches into mosques! Islam, at least

Holds firm in keeping women in their place.
Within her chadhor, every Moslem Mom's
A nun, while *our* nuns change their habits for
A warrior garb of pants and pantyhose.
What we must do, what we have long discussed,
Is to relight the Inquisition's torch
For the instruction and delight of those
Who still can be relied on to attend
Autos-da-fé. Burn down the clinics of
Planned Parenthood. Make foetuscide a crime
Punishable, like homicide, by death,
And if the civil power's craven courts
Should balk, if legislation's voted down
Or overthrown, then we must urge our flocks
To act upon their own. One simple, just
Expedient would be to institute
Homes where reluctant mothers might be brought
To term; initially, for Catholic girls
Whose parents can coerce such penitence,
As once defiant daughters might be placed
In convents; then, that precedent secure,
Encourage a clandestine brotherhood
To save those foetuses whose mothers may
Reject more mild persuasion. Civil crimes
Are justified—read any casuist—
When one is acting in a Higher Cause.
Not that such deeds would make states change their laws:
We would be martyred, made pariahs, sent
To jail—but what a triumph for the rights
Of foetuses, and what a way to weed
The Church's fields of tares. You think I jest:
So did the bishops gathered in St. Louis,
Though after the formalities, Malone
Of Boston and Passaic's Muggerone
Took me aside and asked to know if such
A league of fetal-rights revengers had
Been formed, assuring me that when it was,
They could supply recruits. Then Muggerone
Bewailed the evils of the media,
Who had exposed his till-then secret charity

In bailing out three youths who'd raped and stabbed
A cyclist in the park. The Bishop swears
He acted only in the interest
Of inter-racial harmony, a cause
That also prompted him to champion
St. Athanasius' Orphanage
For Children Born with AIDS, a charity
That has been universally acclaimed
Except by Bishop Muggerone's *bête noir*,
The *Jersey Star*, which claims the charges paid
To the contracting firm of Muggerone
And Sons for laying the foundation of
The orphanage would have sufficed to build
A concrete pyramid upon the site.
It seems the Bishop's outlays for cement
Exceed the county's. He was furious.
"The media!" he roared—and you could see
His chins all in a tremble—"The media
Is killing us. It's Jews is what it is.
Jews hate Italians and control the news.
If you're Italian then you're in the mob.
There is no mob, the mob's a media myth!"
And all the while he fulminates and rants,
His limousine is waiting in the lot,
His chauffeur sinister as some Ton-ton
Macoute. What is so wonderful about
The Bishop is the man's unswerving and
Unnerving righteousness, his perfect Faith
That his shit and the shit of all his kin
Must smell like roses. God, what strength of mind!
Can you suppose that like aggressiveness
Would not more suit the present circumstance
Than to require this pusillanimity
Of me, those mewling statements to the press,
My sanctuary in a drying tank:
As well embroider double A's on alb,
Dalmatic, chasuble, and pallium.
Does Rome believe such sops will satisfy
The public's appetite for blood? I face
A statutory minimum of ten!

And what is being done? I must put by
My crozier, cease to preach from my own pulpit,
Surrender the archdiocese accounts,
As though I were another Muggerone,
Fold my hands and wait for sentencing!
I may not even speak in privacy
With my attorneys, but the legate's spy
Is crouching in the corner taking notes.
You keep me virtually a prisoner:
No telephone, no visitors, no mail
That doesn't bear the Abbot's imprimatur.
And then you counsel me to fast and pray!
Well, I'll be damned if I'll be put away
As docilely as that. I'll bleat before
I bleed. You think *my* case is scandalous?
Wait till the papers get on yours, my boys!
I trust this is a live broadcast, and that
The Abbot's at his intercom—with whom
Else? Let me guess: Monsignor Mallachy;
My Deputy-Archbishop Sneed; and Rome's
Own damage control team, nameless to me.
If I'm not addressing empty air,
And if you'd like to hear the aria
Through to the end, I would appreciate
A dollop of some better lubricant.
I wait Your Graces' pleasure, and my own.

He finishes the last of the wine in the bottle on the tray, then goes to the prie-dieu, kneels, and folds his hands in prayer. The Brother regards him balefully; the Cardinal lowers his eyes. The Brother cocks his head, and presses his hand to his cowl, as though better to listen to earphones. With a look of disgruntlement, he nods and takes the tray with bottle and glass from the room.

Almost as soon as the Brother is out the door, the Cardinal gets the hiccoughs. He goes through various contortions trying to stop hiccoughing, sucking in his gut, holding his breath. He still has the hiccoughs when the Brother returns with a new bottle. The hiccoughs continue for a while even after his first careful sip of wine—each one being indicated by an asterisk within parentheses in the text he speaks: (*).

THE CARDINAL:

Hiccoughs always make me (*) think of Gene
Pacelli, Pius Twelfth, who died of them
And now is offered as a candidate
For sainthood. A saint who can't stop (*) hiccoughing!
As well a holy arsonist, a saint
With clap, a blessed ex(*)ecutioner.
The present Abbot's predecessor felt
A special reverence for his (*) witheredness,
I understand, and entertained the hope
Of a mir(*)aculous remission. Yes?
It must be either Pius has no pull
With God, or sodomites can't win (*) his ear.
Imagine if his prayer'd been answered and
Instead of (*) what it is, a jail for drunks
In Roman collars, the Abbey here became
The (*) Lourdes of AIDS-infected clergymen.
I see them now, coming to hang ex (*) votos
At Pius's shrine. The statute's right hand holds
A model of a concentration camp;
The left, a water glass symbolic of
His (*) sufferings.

*In the course of these blasphemies against Pius XII, the Brother has
approached the Cardinal to refill his quickly emptying glass. His indigna-
tion finally is too much for him, and he slaps the Cardinal across the face,
knocking off his glasses. Immediately, remorseful, he is on his knees to
retrieve the glasses and return them to the Cardinal, who after his initial
shock seems pleased to have made a dent in the Brother's composure.*

THE CARDINAL:

                    I think I touched a nerve.
And you did, too: I've stopped the hiccoughing.
I wonder if you might have saved the Pope,
If you'd been there in 1958?
Now don't explode again: keep beating me,
I may seize up, or modify my tune

To something maddeningly bland, as: jazz,
And its potential for the liturgy,
Or else a homily on nuclear arms
And how the bishops must speak up for peace.
Oh, I have bromides in reserve that could
Sedate entire senates and have done so.
It's one of a bishop's most important jobs
To demonstrate to those who wield real power
The Church's ineffectuality
In matters of much consequence. We scold
Bad boys if they make noise, but otherwise
We turn our eyes away. What if the Church
Were to attack the mafia, instead
Of sub-contracting with it, snuggling up
On St. Columbus Day, and saying Mass
At mobsters' funerals? You know as well
As I, the mafia would attack right back
As ruthlessly as any sovereign state.
Look at the drug lords of Colombia,
Where crime and law at last officially
Are one, the shotgun wedding of all time.
Do you think those drug lords don't intend
To decorate their polity with priests?
Their haciendas have not only taps
Of solid gold, but chapels, too, wherein
The Virgin Mother is particularly
Venerated, and with perfect piety.
For in all things relating to the heart
Criminals, poets, madmen, and lovers
Are more in touch with what they feel than we
Whose lives are ruled by prudence. I have been
Assured by Muggerone that Domenic,
His brother, is as staunchly orthodox
As Ratzinger in Rome—the same "Fat Nick"
Who holds the strings to half the rackets on
The Jersey docks. A scandal? Not at all.
Or not according to His Eminence,
Who takes a high, Dantean view of sin.
As, in the *Inferno*, lustful lovers
Are tumble-dried forever in gusts of flame,

Which *are* the lusts that sucked them down to hell,
So Muggerone insists that every crime
Is its own punishment, and prisons are
Superfluous, especially for the rich,
Whose very riches are more punitive,
In a Dantean sense, than time served in
The cloister of a penitentiary.
A lovely theory, is it not, because
Perfectly self-contained: whatever is
Is right, even if it's wrong. Much more than I,
The Bishop's of a sanguine temperament,
Disposed to find in any seeming ill
The silvery linings of Our Savior's will.
In AIDS he sees a triple blessing: First,
As a plague selective of those most accurst;
And then in that it affords a lingering death,
Time for a true repentance to take root,
And for a good confession at the end;
And lastly, he rejoices in its horror,
Betokening the horror of lust itself,
Which violates the temple of the flesh
And now is seen to do so visibly
For the enlightenment of all who might
Be tempted to the sin of sodomy.
The bishop is no less inventive in
Finding a moral advantage in the plague,
So rampant in his own community,
Of drugs. Not only alcohol.

The Cardinal holds out his cup and as the Brother fills it, continues speaking.

THE CARDINAL:

                      We all,
Who celebrate the Mass, find comfort in
The wine that is our Savior's blood. But crack,
As well. In terms of moral theology,
Drugs are a bit of a conundrum—Cheers!—

Since nowhere in the older Tablets of
The Law are drugs, as such, proscribed. Indeed,
Good Catholics imbibed with not a twinge
Of guilt in Prohibition days, and what
Is alcohol if not a drug? This bottle's
Better, by the by. My compliments
To the cellarer. So, where were we?
Oh, yes: is heroin or ecstasy
Or crack *essentially* more wrong than, say,
A bottle of Chardonnay? Not logically:
It is the use to which it's put. And that,
Among the younger felons of our age
Is to release a murderous rage, and rage
Is anger heightened exponentially,
And anger is, like lust, a deadly sin,
Whose deadliness the plague of AIDS reveals.
This can't be the official view of AIDS,
Of course; it wouldn't play well in the press.
Sufficient that we interdict the use
Of prophylactics; sin and nature can
Be counted on to do the rest. The Church
In this is like those foresters who let
A fire sweep unchecked through timberlands,
Then, when the ashes cool, move in to sow
The seedlings they have kept in readiness.
The Church's view is long as His who formed
The rivers, canyons, reefs, and limestone cliffs,
Taught bees, by trial and error, to mold their nests
In tidy hexagons, and teaches man,
As patiently, to follow Natural Law.
I've read somewhere there are historians
Who call the new age dawning on us now
Post-History, a pregnant phrase, and one
Suggestive of that Thousand Years of Peace
St. John foresaw in his Apocalypse.
If this is so, the Church must reassert
Its claim, based on its own long stability,
To be the stabilizer of the new
Homeostatic state, the *Pax vobiscum*
At the end of time. Oh my, this wine

Is mellower than the first. I hope I may
Interpret it as tender of a more
Merciful, accommodating view
Toward the disposition of my case.
The laurels of authorship as little tempt
Me as the palm of martyrdom, but if
I am thrown to the wolves and made to serve
That statutory minimum, I will
Write such a book the Vatican will wish
I'd never sat at her consistories,
Had not been privy to the audits of
The Banco Ambrosiano, nor been sent
On secret missions to the President.
Oh, I have tales to tell, and they exist
Not only in my mortal memory
But in a still unpolished form in vaults
To which my legal counsel has the key—
In the event of my untimely death
They will be published in their present form,
And I assure you, there'll be such a storm
As has not rocked the Church's holy boat
Since presses multiplied what Luther wrote
Like basketfuls of poisoned loaves and fish.
Such cannot be the Hierarchy's wish.
These are my terms: I must retain my See,
My freedom and my Cardinality.
As to the means, ask Bishop Muggerone
What judges currently are selling for.
Now, if you please, I'd like to use a phone.

*The Cardinal comes to stand directly in front of the Brother, who moves
away from the door. The Cardinal tries the door and finds it locked. He
stands for a while, resting his forehead against the locked door, defeated—
and unaware that the Brother, after receiving another message through his
earphones, employs this moment of inattention to introduce poison into the
opened bottle of wine.*

THE CARDINAL:

I see. It is a kind of miracle
When those who have been blind are made to see.
Attorneys can be bought for half the cost
Of the judiciary. Muggerone
Would have known that. My aide-memoire
Can't help me now, if it is where I think.
                    (faces round, smiling)
Well, then, let me drown myself in drink.

*The Brother pours a full glass of the poisoned wine, which the Cardinal
accepts after a moment of hesitation. As at his first taste of the earlier bottle,
he makes a sour face.*

THE CARDINAL:

Between the first glass and this next, the wine
Would seem to have turned sour. Would you agree?
Ah, I forget—you're sworn to abstinence.
My tongue should have been wise as yours. And mute.

*He tosses back all the wine in the glass and holds it out to be refilled. The
last of the wine is poured in the glass.*

THE CARDINAL:

A toast: to my successful autopsy
And to the holy and redeeming blood
Of Christ. May it provide the evidence
To hang the lot of you! In youth I prayed
I might become a martyr for the Faith.
God has too long a memory, too cruel
A wit—which makes Him, come to think of it,
A God that I deserve, and vice versa.

He flinches with the first effect of the poison. The Brother helps him to sit on the edge of the bed. He begins, again, to hiccough, and makes a desperate effort to stop.

THE CARDINAL:

Water, damn you! Get me a glass of (*)

The Brother takes the wineglass, goes to the door, unlocks it, leaves the room, and returns with the glass full of water. The Cardinal, who is doubled with cramps, and hiccoughing, closes his eyes, holds his breath, growing red in the face and takes twenty sips of water. To no avail. The hiccoughing persists. The Cardinal smashes the glass on the floor. He pulls himself to his feet by clawing at the Brother's habit.

THE CARDINAL:

Cure me! You did before, you (*) must again:
I will not die like that damned (*) wop!

The Brother strikes him across the face, knocking off his glasses, but the blow has no effect against the hiccoughs.

THE CARDINAL:

Again!

The Brother uses all his force. The Cardinal falls back across the bed. His face is bloody. His hiccoughs are gone. He is dead. The Brother kneels at the foot of the bed and makes the sign of the cross.

Curtain

from *The Hudson Review*

Difference

◇ ◇ ◇

The jellyfish
float in the bay shallows
like schools of clouds,

a dozen identical—is it right
to call them creatures,
these elaborate sacks

of nothing? All they seem
is shape, and shifting,
and though a whole troop

of undulant cousins
go about their business
within a single wave's span,

every one does something unlike:
this one a balloon
open on both ends

but swollen to its full expanse,
this one a breathing heart,
this a pulsing flower.

This one a rolled condom,
or a plastic purse swallowing itself,
that one a Tiffany shade,

this a troubled parasol.
This submarine opera's
all subterfuge and disguise,

its plot a fabulous tangle
of hiding and recognition:
nothing but trope,

nothing but something
forming itself into figures
then refiguring,

sheer ectoplasm
recognizable only as the stuff
of metaphor. What can words do

but link what we know
to what we don't,
and so form a shape?

Which shrinks or swells,
configures or collapses, blooms
even as it is described

into some unlikely
marine chiffon:
a gown for Isadora?

Nothing but style.
What binds
one shape to another

also sets them apart
—but what's lovelier
than the shapeshifting

transparence of *like* and *as*:
clear, undulant words?
We look at alien grace,

unfettered
by any determined form,
and we say: balloon, flower,

heart, condom, opera,
lampshade, parasol, ballet.
Hear how the mouth,

so full
of longing for the world,
changes its shape?

from *Boulevard*

Bulimia

◇　◇　◇

A kiss has nothing to do with sex,
she thinks. Not really. That engulfing, that trying to take
all of another in for nourishment, to become one with her, to become
part of her cells. The way she must have had everything she wanted
in the womb, without asking. Without words,
kisses have barely the slurp-sound of a man entering a woman
or sliding back out—neither movement with even the warning of
      a bark.
The Greek word "buli," animal hunger.
Petting, those kisses are called, or sometimes necking.
She read this advice in a sex manual once: "Take the man's penis,
slowly at first, like you are licking melting ice cream
from the rim of a cone." But the gagging, the choke—
a hot gulp of tea, a small chicken bone, a wad of gum grown too big.
That wasn't mentioned. It's about what happens in her mouth
past her teeth, where there is no more control, like a waterfall—
or its being too late when the whole wedding cake is gone:

She orders one from a different bakery this time, so no one
will remember her past visits and catch on. She's eating
slowly at first, tonguing icing from the plastic groom's feet, the hem
of the bride's gown, and those toothpick-points that kept them
rooted in pastry. She cuts the top tier into squares,
reception-like. (The thrill she knew of a wedding this past June,
stealing the white dessert into her purse, sucking
the sugary blue gel from a napkin one piece was wrapped in.
She was swallowing paper on her lone car ride home,
through a red light, on her way to another nap
from which she hoped a prince's kiss would wake her.)

The second tier in her hands, by fistfuls, desperate
as the Third World child she saw on tv last week, taking in gruel.
Her head, light like her stomach is pumped up with air.
She can't stop. She puckers up to the sticky crumbs under her nails.
Then there are the engraved Valentine candies:
CRAZY, DREAM GIRL, ACT NOW, YOU'RE HOT. She rips open the bag,
devouring as many messages as she can at once.
They all taste like chalk. She rocks back and forth.

She has to loosen the string on her sweat pants, part of her trousseau.
The bag of candy is emptied. The paper doily
under the cake's third layer, smooth as a vacuumed ice-skating rink.
What has she done? In the bathroom, like what happened

to the mistakenly flushed-away bracelet, a gift
from her first boyfriend—the gold clasp silently unhooking
as she wiped herself, then, moments too late, noticing
her naked wrist under the running water of the rest room
sink's faucet . . . She's learned it's best to wait ten minutes
to make herself throw up. Digestion begins at this point,
but the food hasn't gotten very far. As ingenious as the first
few times she would consciously masturbate, making note of where
her fingers felt best, she devises a way to vomit
that only hurts for a second.

She takes off her sweatshirt and drapes it over a towel rack.
Then she pokes a Q-Tip on her soft palate. Keeping in mind
the diagram in her voice class, the cross section
of the mouth showing each part's different function,
the palate—hidden and secret as a clitoris.
The teacher's mentioning of its vulnerability, split-second
and nonchalant like a doctor and his tongue depressor.
It's a fast prayer—she kneels in front of the toilet.
Her back jerks and arches the way it might
if she were moving her body to meet a man's during intercourse.
She wipes what has sprayed back to her chest,
her throat as raw as a rape that's happened to someone else.
She cleans the seat of the bowl with a rag, and cleans
her teeth with a second toothbrush she keeps for this purpose.
Her sweatshirt back on, she gets to the kitchen

to crush the cake box into a plastic garbage bag.
And leaves to dispose of it, not in the trashcan downstairs,
but in a dumpster way on the other side of town.

from *Poet Lore*

TONY ESOLEN

Northwestern Mathematics

◇   ◇   ◇

Hard to say what the natural numbers are.
A lot of ones: the snowy falcon, floating
Like god over the vast northwest, alone
Until the only ptarmigan pokes her head
From her rock cover; one mink in a trap,
His innocent tracks forever. Twos and threes
Crop up, now and again. Teenagers veering
Over to Fort Smith on their snowmobiles,
To hang like wolves around the Wine and Dine,
Jukeboxes, soaked boots, beer, big waitresses.
Two bucks for orange juice. The scuttlebutt:
Sheila and Gray Sky and her slapstick husband.
That's life. Another round. And you can reach
Up to thirteen, in the jock-sweat fishing shack
Of Lester Manatu & Sons. You rent
An outboard, fine, Manatu nods and doesn't
Bother to mark you down; his oldest grandson
Tallies up the accounts, keeps him in booze;
The old man, stubborn, stalls at seventy.
He's on the books as Presbyterian, but
He never bothered much with books, or words,
And she's long dead who once could make him sing.
He hauls his tackle box like a limb grown
Evergreen out of him these many years.
He likes me well enough, but he won't speak
Other than ordinal words: here, hold this, wait.
He walks off to the limit of the world
To test, I don't know what, the ice, the weather,
An elk-trail molten into nothing. Life

Is what he moves in, my old hand at winter,
Life like the sweep of sky and plain his figure
Vanishes into, with the scattered bloom
Of a few numbers, and continuum.

from *Fine Madness*

Life Drawing

◊　◊　◊

The model stands in the pale composure of his nakedness
　　where sunlight has chiseled him from shadow
　　　　like a kouros striding out of stone.

On the dais, apart, he is a locus of stillness and power,
　　without modesty or name, with no presence
　　　　other than the specificity of flesh

the eye can render with hard Euclidean curves.
　　The taut musculature of his abdomen and thighs,
　　　　the languid sex and gaze—all the impediments

of time—he bares before the world, as if they were miracles
　　intended to disrupt this moment's purity
　　　　and the paper's immaculate void.

from *Poetry*

The Priming Is a Negligee

◊ ◊ ◊

between the oils and canvas. Stroke the white
sheath well into the weave. The canvas
needs more veil. The painting
　　　　　　　　should float on skins of lead
white coating—or its oils will wither
the linen they touch, its colors gnaw
at cloth until the image hangs on air.
　　　　　The canvas needs more veil.

　　　　　　　The body takes its own shade
with it everywhere. There are true gessos
　　　　　flesh will accept: blocks and screens
to keep the sun just out of reach. Creams
　　　　white as Styrofoam but less
perpetual, vanishing like varnish
once they're crammed between the cells.
　　　　　So skin is sheltered
　　　　　　　　by transparencies, iced
with positive shadows. Sunshade.
The nihilist is light.
　　　　　　　Printers know it's the leading

between lines that lets them be
swaddled in the rag of stanzas.
How close the letters huddle
　　　　without rubbing. For immersion see
"passion between." See

opposite of serene. For synonym and homonym
see "rapt" and "wrapped."
       There is a gown—that breathes—

and a gown—that heats. One to hold,
                         one to release. Watch
the lead white camisole go up
       in arms and hair and skin.
That one flings it like a shiny jelly
       to the floor. With beautiful frugality, go
the solid cotton briefs.
       The lovers get so excited

to think—nothing comes between them.
                         There is nothing between them.
That's how they can consume each other,
       sand each other sore.
The oils are suspended
       on a leading. The lovers
touch in linen walls.

       from *Southwest Review*

After Dark

◇ ◇ ◇

She is thinking of the delta
shimmering with tidal and fresh water urgings

as his hand opens on the flat
of her breast bone. So much sediment

there, the Mississippi argues its way
through the bayous, pausing for the ibis,

the tall-legged cypress, the heron
that cannot decide, walking backwards,

it seems while moving ahead.
A million years of water

in which sturgeon, carp and crustacean
sink and rise with the leaves

of the ancient willow,
half-dissolved root, pungent bone.

In this ambiguous world, both fluid
and firm, she drifts between the blurry borders

of the current, and beyond,
through cottonwood nebulas, pollen, and siftings

of alluvial plain, admitting
love can exceed our intentions,

those levees built against flooding.
But mainly she is struck

by its patient, persistent nature.
The constant nibbling of the river

like a fiddler crab
whose tiny legs (tickling like his beard)

weaken a soft bank until, thunder from afar,
it collapses into water.

from *Poetry*

JORIE GRAHAM

In the Hotel

◊ ◊ ◊

(*3:17 A.M.*)

Whirr. The invisible sponsored again by white
walls—a joining in them and then (dark spot)
(like the start of a thought)
a corner, fertilized by shadow, hooked, dotted,
here demurring, there—up there—
almost hot with black . . . What time is it?
The annihilation. The chaste middle of things.
Then I hear them, whoever they are, as if
inside my wall, as if there were a multitude of tiny wings
                                                        trapped
inside the studs and joints.
The clock dial hums. Greenish glow and twelve stark dots
round which this supple, sinewed, blackest flesh
must roil—vertebrate. A moaning now—a human moan—and then
another cry—but small—
furry in the way the wall can hold it—no
regret—a cry like a hypothesis—another
cry—the first again?—but not as in
dialogue—no—no question in it,
no having heard—now both—no moods in that room—
no fate—cries the precipitate of something on the verge of—
all of it supple now, threadbare in this black we share,
little whelps, vanquishings, discoveries, here under this
                                                        rock,
no, over here, inside this sky, or is it below?—paupers,
                                                        spoors—
a common grave—the backbone still glowing green—

and blackness, and the sense of walls, and the voicing they
provide, and my stillness here—unblinking—I am almost
                                        afraid
to move—and the litheness of this listening—
gossipy murmuring syllables now rushing up the scales,
but not really toward, not really away,
as if the thing deepened without increase,
the weight of the covers upon me,
the weight of the black, the slack and heaving argument
                                of gravity—
and her, quavering, lingering—
and him—what had been mossy
            suddenly clawed—
and everything now trying to arrive on time, ten thousand
                    invisible things all
braided in, fast—*appetite, the clatter of wheels upon tracks,*
the rustling—what did I lose?—what was it
like?—the weight of covers now upon me like the world's
                                shut lid,
shut fast—not opening—
and cries, and cries, and something that will not come true.
When I stand up, pulling the heavy bedclothes back,
I want to open up the black.
Water sounds in the pipes between us.
A raised voice. Some steps.
More water in the singing pipes.
And scuffling. And the clicking of their light going off . . .
Debris of silences inside the silence.
Black gorged with absences. Room like an eyelid
                        spanked open
wide, I rip it, I rip it further—as if inside it now the million
tiny slippages could go to work, the whistling
                    of absence
where the thing *should care for us*—
where justice shifts and reshifts the bits to make
                    tomorrow—
tirelessly—kingdom of scribble and linger. . . . What do you
want, *you*, listening here with me now? Inside the
                        monologue,
what would you insert? What word?

What mark upon the pleating blackness of hotel air?
What, to open it? To make it hear you. To make it hear me.
How heavy can the singleness become?
Who will hear us? What shall we do?
I have waited all this time in the sooty minutes,
green gleaming bouquet offering and offering itself
right to my unrelenting open eyes,
long black arm tendering its icy blossoms up to me,
right through the blizzard of instances, the blurry
blacknesses, the whole room choked with the thousand spots
                              my glance has struck—
Long ago, long ago, and then, secondhand, this place
                              which is now,
whirr—immortal? free?—glances like flames licking the walls . . .
Oh blackness, I am your servant. I take for mine your green,
                              exactest gift
in which you say yourself, in which you say
only yourself—

from *The New Yorker*

The Frog in the Swimming Pool

◇ ◇ ◇

A wet green velvet scums the swimming pool,
furring the cracks. The deep end swims
in a hatful of rain, not enough to float

the bedspring barge, the tug of shopping cart.
Green-wet himself, the bullfrog holds his court,
sounding the summons to a life so low

he's yet to lure a mate. Under the lip
of concrete slab he reigns, a rumble of rock,
a flickering of sticky tongue that's licked

at any morsel winging into view.
How would he love her? Let me count the waves
that scrape the underside of night and then

let go, the depth of love unplumbed, the breadth,
the height of the pool all he needs to know.
How do I love him? Let me add the weight

of one hush to another, the mockingbird
at midnight echoing itself, not him,
one silence torn in two, sewn shut again.

Down to his level in time wings everything.
He calls the night down on his unlovely head,
on the slimy skin that breathes the slimy air—

the skin that's shed and still he is the same,
the first voice in the world, the last each night.
His call has failed to fill the empty house

across the street, the vacant swing that sways
halfheartedly, the slide slid into rust,
the old griefs waiting burial by the new.

from *The New Republic*

DONALD HALL

Another Elegy

◇　◇　◇

In Memory of
William Trout

"O God!" thoughte I, "that madest kynde,
Shal I noon other weyes dye?
Wher Joves woll me stellefye,
Or what thing may this sygnifye? . . ."
Geoffrey Chaucer, *House of Fame*

The task and potential greatness of mortals reside
in their ability to produce things which are at home
in everlastingness.
Hannah Arendt, *The Human Condition*

Both one and many; in the brown baked features
The eyes of a familiar compound ghost . . .
T. S. Eliot, "Little Gidding"

It rained all night on the remaining elms. April soaked
through night loam into sleep. This morning, rain delays
above drenched earth. Whitethroated sparrows shake
wet from their feathers, singing in the oak, while fog
snags like lambswool on Kearsarge. The Blackwater River
runs high. The blacksnake budges in his hole, resurrecting
from winter's coma.

Now green will start from stubble
and horned pout fatten. By the pond, pussywillows
will labor awake to trudge from darkness and cold
through April's creaking age.
                    Bill Trout remains
fixed in a long box where we left him, a dozen years ago.

*

July, nineteen sixty: Three friends with their families
visited Bill at his Maine cabin secluded among scrub pines—
setting up tents, joking, frying pickerel in cool dusk.

Only Bill was divorced, drinking all night, living alone
on his shabby acre. Drunk the whole week, he recited
Milton's syllables of lament, interrupting our argument,
told Nazarene parables, and wept for his friends
and their children. While the rest of us dove from a dock
or played badminton with our wives, Bill paced
muttering, smoking his Lucky Strikes. Later the rest
divorced and paced.
                    We fished the river for horned pout,
Bill standing with a joint by the dam, watching the warm
water thick with fish, black bodies packed, flapping
and contending to breathe. Dropping hooks without bait,
we pulled up the horny, loricate fish, then flipped them
on grass to shrivel as we watched and joked, old
friends together. Continually sloshed, Bill proclaimed
that life was shit, death was shit—even *shit* was *shit*.

*

Idaho made him, Pocatello of hobos and freightyards—
clangor of iron, fetor of coalsmoke. With his brothers
he listened for the Mountain Bluebird as he dropped worms
into the Snake River, harvesting catfish for a Saturday
supper in the nineteen thirties.

Two Sisters of the Sacred Heart
cossetted him when he strayed from the boys' flock
to scan the unchanging dactyls of Ovid. Landowska set out
the Goldberg Variations on a hand-wound Victrola.

When he was fifteen he stayed home from fishing to number
feet that promenaded to a Union Pacific tune, ABAB
pentameters. At the university his teacher the disappointed
novelist nodded his head—in admiration, envy, and pity—
while Bill sat late at a yellow dormitory desk, daydreaming
that his poems lifted through night sky to become stars
fixed in heaven, as Keats's poems rose from Hampstead
lanes and talks with Hunt and Haydon.
                                        When he considered
the cloth, Bill saw himself martyred. The ambition
of priest and poet!—innocent, and brainless as a shark.

★

Sculptors make models for touch; singers raise voices
to the possible voice; basketball players improvise
humors of levitation. They jump, carve, and sing in plain
air as we do dreaming.
                        Because emblems of every calling
measure its aspiration, the basketball player shoots
three hundred freethrows before breakfast; the mezzo
exists in service to the sound she makes, without eating
or loving except for song, selfish and selfless together;
the novice imagines herself healing a dozen Calcuttas
as Mother Teresa smiles from a gold cloud, and violates
holiness by her daydream of holiness.
                                        Bill Trout
woke up, the best mornings of his life—without debilities
of hangover, without pills or panic—to practice joy
at four o'clock dawn: to test words, to break them down
and build again, patient to construct immovable objects
of art by the pains of intelligent attention—remaining
alert or awake to nightmare.

But the maker of bronzes
dies decapitated in the carwreck; the whitefaced mime
dozes tied to the wheelchair; the saint babbles and drools;
carcinoma refines chemist, farmer, wino, professor, poet,
imbecile, and banker into a passion of three nerves
and a feeding tube.
　　　　　At the Bayside Hospice Bill's body
heaved as it worked for air; IVs dripped; bloody phlegm
boiled from the hole punched like a grommet in his throat.

★

Another fisherman writes me: "A man's death is his own;
you take Bill's death away, for public tears." I remember
Bill depressed, drinking double Manhattans straight up,
taunting himself: "Compassion's flack! Elmer Gantry
of Guggenheim grief!" In Coleridge's *Notebooks*,
he underlined: "Poetry—excites us to artificial feelings—
callous to real ones."
　　　　　　　Commonly Bill recited, from John 14,
"I go to make a place," then shrugged and sang the Wobbly
hymn, "You'll eat pie in the sky by and by—when you die."
After reciting Thomas Hardy, he went on to mimic Oliver.

Two years after the Maine summer, he worked for SNCC
in Alabama, in a cadre of Christians and Jews, beaten bloody
and jailed, declaiming Amos as gospel of anger and love.

Angry he married again; loving he wrote "Selma with Hellfire."

A decade after, as we sat late in a bare Port Townsend room,
bossily I reminded him to eat the wax-paper'd hamburger
cooling by his ashtray. Bill delivered a line, in his voice
as lush as an old Shakespearean's: "Ohhh . . . to think
of the mornings I've waked with a cold cheeseburger beside me!"

He walked into water and out again; he woke in the drunktank
heaving; he trembled after electroshock; he made the poems.

★

If ambition is innocent, nevertheless it impairs those
it possesses, not to mention their irretrievable children.

In the interstices of alcohol and woe, Bill vibrated
awake to a room that surged, shook, and altered shape.
He secreted vowel-honey in images dangling from prepositions;
he praised survival.
When he finished his sojourn
at McLean, where Very and Lowell had paced before him;
when Margaret left him, removing their daughter, and Bill
declared bankruptcy; when he was unable for five years
to take Communion—he drank two Guggenheims and snorted
an NEA. He quoted Amos: ". . . as if a man fled from a lion
and a bear met him."
From his house in Oakland, USIS
flew him to Prague, then home to detox. Once I visited him
just back from drying out, shuffling from chair to table
like a ninety-year-old, shaking as he tried to light
his Lucky, barely able to speak.
Then in middle age
he fell in love again. He listened again to Chaucer
and recited Spenser's refrain as he stood by the Thames,
holding his Hindu love by the hand; or walking arm in arm
by a lake where Wordsworth walked;
or, happy in Delhi,
reading the Gita, he breathed each morning India's fetid
exhausted air, filling his notebook in warm dawn
as parrots flashed and his throat opened with gold
vowels, line after beautiful line, all the last summer.

*

The week before he died he handed me a clutch of poems.
Speechless, syllables occluded in his throat, he raised
a yellow pad and wrote, "That's it." Eyes protruded
from bone sockets; neck cords strained; trunk heaved
as he looked for his love who gazed out the window
of the room, bare except for a crucifix, downward to the bay
and the brown edges of March.

After he died Reba gave me
his Modern Library Dickinson, in which editors corrected
the poet's lines. I imagine Bill in Eugene, penciling,
neat in the margin, restorations of Amherst.
                                                    Each year
his death grows older. Outside this house, past Kearsarge
changing from pink and lavender through blue and white
to green, public language ridicules "eager pursuit of honor."

Do I tell lies? ". . . in middle age he fell in love . . ."
Did he never again tremble from chair to table? At night
Bill delivered his imagination and study to *Laverne*
and Shirley, laughing when a laughtrack bullied him
to laugh—while Reba groaned an incredulous Bengali groan—
in order not to drink.
                                Yet again he walked in a blue
robe in detox, love's anguish and anger walking beside him.

★

It is twelve Aprils since we buried him. Now dissertation-
salt preserves *The Collected Poems of William Trout*
like Lenin. Here is another elegy in the tradition
of mourning and envy, love and self-love—as another morning
delivers rain on the fishbone leaves of the rotted year.
Again I measure the poems Bill Trout left on the shore
of his scattery life: quatrains that scrubbed Pocatello
clean, numbers of nightmare and magic, late songs in love
with Reba and vowels—his lifelines that hooked and landed
himself and his own for his book.
                                            But if a new fixed star
resurrects Bill's words who labored and excelled, not even
Chaucer's or Ovid's accomplishment—"Joves woll me stellyfye"—
will revise electrodes, jail, and death at fifty.
Bill Trout is incorrigible, like the recidivist blacksnake,
sparrow, and high water that turn and return in April's
versions—cycles of the same, fish making fish—

                                                          "unless,"
Bill dying, shriveled and absolved, wrote on a yellow
pad, "Jesus who walked from the tomb has made a place."

                          from *The Iowa Review*

Getting Happy

◊　◊　◊

When the men got happy in church,
　　they shouted and jumped straight up.

But the women's trances
　　made them dance with moaning; so,

I dreaded Rev. Johnson's sermons
　　near their end, hated the trouble

he was causing inside
　　the souls of women sweating

and beginning to breathe fast.
　　One day, I worried, my mother

would let go and lose herself
　　to him, become as giddy

as when my father was coming home
　　on leave. Just as silly.

Yet, when it finally happened,
　　I felt only left behind.

Years later, another first time,
　　I heard my moan echo inside

a girl's ear and recognized
　　how woeful pleasure feels.

I then began to wonder
   if there weren't some joy still

to give in to, make me shout
   not as men do but as a woman.

It troubles me.
   I do not have a woman's body

but fear that moaning will betray
   this want in me, or of another

to be like a woman. Mostly,
   I fear that moaning will uncover

the love for my mother that is still
   so deep that I want little more

than to be with her as closely as I can.

from *ZYZZYVA*

The Polar Circle

◇　◇　◇

for Lauri Nykopp

The world is between tips
We say so to know
We go to look over or out to its pivot, to its
    wobble and drift
Terrible
We are leaving
There's nothing to come to there but
    transformation and tint
Seductions
So we can't be repeating
What one knows in this state can't be known in
    another
Time matches nothing

People don't circle, certainly not unless they are
    responsible
But sleeps pine or eagle or tide to gratify
And thousands depend on one
Repeated
And all that's repeated is mediated
Thought
The order is such that it situates
At the farthest extent of a scene are its
    reachings
Night life is search of its kind
Hands open and fingers shuffle

I could gesture not of persons but of crevice,
      preface, and prelude
I imagine without standpoint poised at loss point
At pole
I easily sleep in its entered light but don't
      write
It doesn't behoove me to make myself smaller than
      I am
And the horizon doesn't hold there
It isn't grained
Its gaping point of contact spreads the latitudes
The pole is interminable, coming and going as if
      solely on rock
But it isn't singular
It shares the mobility of an oblivion I want to
      witness

The world looks like
The pole draws the whirlpools
And to express scope one turns the top of one's
      head
In time the berries unfold of nothing but gold
      cloud
Every color is gathered and then flown
We were even in the red bogs—everything is always
      even
The rivers were amber as tea
And I didn't want to tell, though I seemed to
I always wanted what has no beginning but not what
      has no end
There must be point and it might be tide
Time—North
I think of reason everywhere and it overlaps
Reasonable eventuality and long partition—
      grammar, supper, and sleep ideas are chasing
To pole
It says the dog joined in and tore off the whole
      of a man's face while the man, his arms
      clasped round its back, broke every bone in

the dog's body, and there the pair of them
lay, dead, seizing what seemed to be the only
chance

We dream with our limbs on our heads
As Poe says, It is a happiness to wonder
Our ankles are the hottest
It is happiness to dream
The men ask me where is the charred pot and I say
        it is in the car trunk
The men deny that the slopes have walked into the
        creek
They are probably right and keep consuming
Fire they need—they who come in and fall to their
        knees
To ground

Human curiosity contradicts the human will to
        believe
Before going north I almost had been stopping
But what's the denial of solving
Night visions rhyme—peaks, language, sleep,
        light, tundra, lichen
Because of the obscurity of such phenomena Nature
        seems uncanny
It lets us mock and destroy the utterly complete
Sleep is what remains of Nature
That merely mathematical recognition of equality,
        Poe says, which seems to be the root of all
        beauty
With night thoughts like these, are we not
        logicians
The lower teeth fall out and point saying,
        "Ourselves!"
We are barbarian, recalcitrant, in sleep
Probably we sleep beyond our strength
But what has happened?
As herself at the Arctic limit I would leave
        myself

Still I ask, "Am I contributing something?"
A sleeper leaning over more than ever to make
    contact with reality
Everything is scattered beyond the face
Detached
But persons have their immortality to sacrifice—
    and why stop?

from *Grand Street*

Deceptively Like a Solid

◇　◇　◇

The conference is on Glass, in
Montreal. Wintry light declines
to penetrate windows, and soon
will be lit glass-enclosed glows
so that we may talk, talk into
the night (fortified by bottled
mineral waters), of the metric
of order trespassing on prevailing
chaos that gives this warder
of our warmed up air, clinker,
its viscous, transparent strength.

The beginning was, is
silica, this peon stuff
of the earth, in quartz,

cristoballite, coesite,
stishovite. Pristine marching
bands of atoms

(surpassing the names we give
them) build crystalline lattices
from chains, rings, of Si

alternating with oxygen,
each silicon tetrahedrally
coordinated

by O's, each oxygen
ion, so different from the
life-giving, inflaming

diatomic gas, joining
two silicons; on to rings
in diamondoid

perfection in cristoballite;
helical O–Si–O chains
in quartz, handed in

coiling, mirror images
of each other, hard, ionic
SiO_2.

There must be reasons for such
perfection—time lent to the
earth: then lava

flowed, the air blew thicker, still
no compound or simple eye
to fret defect

into the ur–liquid from which silica
crystallized. But in time we did
come, handy, set

to garner sand, limestone, soda
ash, to break the still witness
of silica. Heat

disrupts. Not the warmth of
Alabama midsummer
evenings, not your hand

but formless wonder of pro-
longed fire, the blast of air drawn
in, controlled fire

storms. Sand, which is silica,
melts. To a liquid, where
order is local

but not long-range. Atoms wander
from their places, bonds break,
tetrahedra

in a tizzy, juxtapose, chains tilt,
bump and stretch—Jaggerwalky.
The restive structures

in microscopic turmoil
meld to gross flow, bubbling
eddies of the melt.

Peace in crystal meshes, peace
in hot yellow flux. But the gloved
men who hold the ladles
get nervy volcanoes
on their minds. So—tilt, pour . . .
douse, so quench,
freeze in that micro lurch.
Glass forms,
and who would have thought it clear?

We posit that the chanced,
in its innards so upset, ought
not be transparent. Light
scattered from entangled polymer
blocks, adventitious dirt,
owes it to us—oh, we see it
so clearly—to lose its way,
come awash in black or at
least in the muddy browns
of spring run-off, another flux.

But light's submicroscopic
tap dance is done in place.

The crossed fields shimmer,
resonant, they plink
electron orbits of O and Si.
Atoms matter, their neighbors
less, the tangle of the locked-in
liquid irrelevant in the
birthing of color, or lack of it.

Optical fibers   Crystal Palace
        The Worshipful Company of Glass Sellers
recycled   Millefiori
prone to shattering   Prince Rupert's drops
Chartres, Rouen, Amiens   float
Pyrex   Vycor   glass wool
network modifiers   the Palomar mirror
smoked for viewing eclipses   thermos
lead glass   microcrack
etched with hydrofluoric acid   spun
frustration   bull's eyes   annealed
borosilicate   softening point

High winds on Etna or Kilauea
spin off the surface
of a lava lake thin fibers.
Pele's hair.
The Goddess's hair,
here black.

                from *Glass Technology*

Variations on a Fragment by Trumbull Stickney

◇   ◇   ◇

I hear a river thro' the valley wander
Whose water runs, the song alone remaining.
A rainbow stands and summer passes under,

Flowing like silence in the light of wonder.
In the near distances it is still raining
Where now the valley fills again with thunder,

Where now the river in her wide meander,
Losing at each loop what she had been gaining,
Moves into what one might as well call yonder.

The way of the dark water is to ponder
The way the light sings as of something waning.
The far-off waterfall can sound asunder

Stillness of distances, as if in blunder,
Tumbling over the rim of all explaining.
Water proves nothing, but can only maunder.

Shadows show nothing, but can only launder
The lovely land that sunset had been staining,
Long fields of which the falling light grows fonder.

Here summer stands while all its songs pass under,
A riverbank still time runs by, remaining.
I will remember rainbows as I wander.

from *The Paris Review*

The Love of the Flesh

◇　◇　◇

Reality is not limited to the tactile:
still, we touch our own faces, as if by the slide
of fingers over cheekbones, eyelids, lips,

we can check that we are not dreaming. This is
the life of the body, the life of gesture,

tangible, a palm against the skin.
When I put my hand to your face it becomes a caress,
but here, against my own, it is disbelief
or wonder.

The questions are hard, as when medieval scholars
divvied up the body in debate
as to where the soul hung its ephemeral hat—

and those who plumped for the heart laboring its fenced-in field
shouted down those others who felt God's messages
precisely in the pit of the stomach,

while the ancients reasoned *the brain, the unromantic brain,*
and virtually every organ had its champion . . .

Their filigree of argument confounds me
just as, then,
the suddenness of love left me dazed:

for days they had to call me twice
to get a single answer—I was deaf
and breathless and stunned. It was not
as if the world were new and beautiful.

It was, instead, as if I had unlearned
how to use my hands
and feet. Where does the life of the body

leave off, the life of the spirit start? When
does the mouthful of air move beyond breathing
towards magic? We made

a spectacle of ourselves, dancing about
like clowns in huge shoes, goofy with happiness,
inarticulate in all but the lexicon
of sexual flesh;

and the soul, from its short-leased home
among the muscles, sent its respects,
or so we were told . . .

Even in *Paradise*, the light-filled spirits
long for their resurrection,
and Dante is surprised that they miss their bodies:

"Not only for themselves," he speculates,
"but for their mothers and fathers, and for the others
dear to them on earth,"

souls wistful for flesh, nostalgic
for their faraway, simple selves who walked about

and who, lifting and seeing their hands,
thought suddenly one day *These touch, caress, stroke;*
who found in the body a bridge beyond it

and coined the word *beloved.* And thus we performed
for ourselves the seamless changing over
of element to element,

body to air, solid to spirit, magic trick
or miracle, without knowing the particular
spell or prayer or luck that made it quicken.

from *Tar River Poetry*

Baseball

◊　◊　◊

When the world finally ends,
a baseball will be hovering
over a diamond somewhere in New Jersey:
a flash of flesh falling out of its clothes
and suddenly no one's there.
The baseball, singed and glowing,
drops to the ground again.
But let's back up twenty years or so.
It's the 1970's and the Oakland A's
have 19th Century faces,
as if they'd stepped from a Balzac novel
belatedly in spring.
A dynasty of troublesome players
who like to fight and slide,
they've just won their third World Series
but trip on their long hair
and wear Edwardian clothes,
the messy but dressy look.
Back then, I'd lie in bed all day,
watching the Cubs and Watergate
on a black and white TV.
Then I'd get up, write some poems,
and pick the goldfish off the floor,
which liked to leap from its tank
because the kissing gouramis
would suck pink holes in its sides.
The poems were not about kissing
but had a violent side,
the way a man's gaze can be "violent,"

fixing you into an object
that, while it lacks a "lack,"
stands up like a fetish.
You feel your face go rubber,
as if your body were filling
with grief. Meanwhile, Reggie Jackson,
while not completely phallocentric,
did create a firm impression
as he "stroked" the ball
for a homer. Sometimes
he flailed and fell, but now
he's out of ball. Left-handedness
is a sinister business, but in
the major leagues, you want
a few of these wizards
on first base or the mound.
Does "mound" have a sexual sound?
And what about "stick men"?
Baseball in the movies—
for instance *Field of Dreams*—
is basically conservative,
says Pauline Kael and one agrees:
"Play ball" is the message,
the dream of male tradition
passing and to come. Besides,
those uniforms, so quasi-pseudo-
semi-demi-military in fashion.
They make us watch them swing
their sticks, slide between
another man's legs, as if
that torso heaven were all
the spit we're worth, we who
sit and dream, eat and talk,
as gulls stir over the field.
I like to watch the grass,
a simple wedge of astonishment
each time I enter the park.
Then the boffo noise of the crowd
clucks and drones like an engine.
I want a hot dog now! And beer

to spill down concrete steps.
My goodness, some of those guys
actually look like gods!
And some of them look just
upwardly mobile, tossing a wink
at their accountants Horvath,
Perkins, Wiggins, and Peal.
One imagines the Yankee Clipper,
smooth as smoke, crossing an outfield of fog.
Lou Gehrig stands at the mike,
saying an iron goodbye, and Babe Ruth
points at the fence where the ball
will probably go if all the myths
were right. Here's Pepper Martin
putting his spikes in your face,
Dizzy Dean's elegant rasp
as he chews a point with Pee Wee Reese.
I remember when Cincinnati
had Birdie Tebbetts, Dusty Rhodes,
Vada Pinson, and Ted Kluszewski.
The sponsor was Hudepohl beer,
and they played in Crosley Field.
The man sitting next to us
waved a gun whenever a run was scored,
then put it back in his girlfriend's
purse. We thought that was fine.
Claes Oldenburg insists
baseball is an "aesthetic game,"
all that flutter of color
creating the eye when strict rows
randomly move. But "poetry in motion"?
I can't say I believe. Poetry
comes in your mouth like flesh;
it rises to the surface
like a ball held underwater,
bouncing a little but staying there,
hardly transcendental but present
nevertheless. You watch it watching you,
staying and going, the silk
suck of a curtain that seems

to leave the building by way
of a window one day, then slips
back over the sill because a door
was opened. Its absolute feet
aren't there, disappearing like
a corner the moment you approach.
Baseball, on the other hand,
presents itself like air,
love's green moment still,
at two in the afternoon.

from *Another Chicago Magazine* and *Witness*

RICHARD HOWARD

A Lost Art

◊ ◊ ◊

Vienna, 1805

There is no ceremony to stand on,
just walk in! No call to be dismayed:
it is not chaos you see in my shop,
but the leavings of creation; nothing
can do you any harm, and nothing is
so far along that you'll do harm to *it* . . . .

Suppose you sit—just put that on the floor—
over here . . . . Never mind, I can fix it:
legs are the least of my difficulties,
there! Welcome to the land of the missing,
where little is past recall. Or repair.
This? Oh, this is my *first* capybara,

I persuaded a chamberlain I know
at the Palace—whom you may know as well,
he's been up there for years, for *dynasties*:
Herr Pufendorf?—to let me have it back,
once I had pledged myself to substitute
a more convincing representative.

No, no, the eyes are set too high, and *green*!
a libel on the living article . . . .
I keep it here, fallacious as it is,
to remind me, in a cautionary way,
that I can do (and have done) better work.
I have long since eclipsed such things, rising

from capybara to *homo capax:*
honest progress. A pity you cannot
confirm my boast; a word to Pufendorf,
not so long since, would have afforded you
the sight of my *magnum opus,* displayed
in the Imperial Museum—kept out

for years, just standing there in . . . state,
I have been told, in spite of protests from
the poor man's family. Not Pufendorf—
he has no family, to my knowledge!
"Poor man" refers to our black Angelo
Solyman, who was to be seen entire,

naked from head to heels, and all between,
the upshot of my labor and my skill . . . .
It would have been no trick at all to do
a costumed figure, just the face and hands
set off by the white court dress, the gold braid,
the medals he invariably wore;

quite another matter to show the man's . . .
manhood, as my commission specified;
why, just to gain possession of the corpse
was a crime! Or would have been, if I'd
been caught: stolen at birth, stolen at death—
a slave's fate, for the honors bestowed.

Then came the wife's compunction—she had been
widowed by a Flemish general and
married to Solyman in secret rite,
though in St. Stephen's Cathedral. Yet
not even the Cardinal-Archbishop
could baffle the Emperor's plan. And I?

I did as I was ordered, did my best:
I allude to the *new* Emperor, of course,
not our late Joseph, who abhorred the sight

of stuffed animals of any species
(the entire Imperial family
suffered from this . . . susceptibility,

until Francis—in so many respects
the converse of his uncle). Now Francis,
Solyman safely dead, commanded me
to prepare, preserve, and present him
as a perfect specimen *in all respects.*
He meant, of course, *in one:* I was to find

a way of representing what is held
to be the special virtue of black men,
although, however . . . outstanding in life,
our man's endowments were, most likely, dimmed
by being dead, revived in part, and stuffed!
Moreover he had died quite civilly—

no evidence from the gibbet would grant
a hint of eventual scope to my art
nor any sculptor's manual of scale
suggest a means of reckoning how much
I might have to contend with. And I could
hardly ask the wronged widow for details!

An old cookery-book delivered me:
by gently passing oil of cloves, it said,
over the affected body parts . . . . Well,
even in the coldest larder, it seems,
an ox's member could be coaxed to life
or at least to life's dimensions, for a while.

And so it came about that Solyman—
born a prince in Pangusitlong, raised
a slave by robbers in Messina, sold
to one General Lobkowitz, by whom
he was bequeathed to Prince von Liechtenstein
who freed and later pensioned him for life—

A Mason, moreover, in Mozart's Lodge
(where both attended assiduously!)
who spoke German, Italian, English, French,
an excellent player of faro and chess,
observed in Frankfurt by the adolescent
Goethe at the Emperor's election—

this very Solyman you might have seen
for yourself in all his mortifying
splendor in the Museum, though of course
what I had studied to produce was more
of a demonstration piece—much visited
by our ladies, and some gentlemen too!—

than any emblem of human headway
in what civilization we may have—
something by way of a memorandum,
actually. No, I never visited:
I did the work, it is gone. Why torment
myself further? I know what I achieved.

I am told that after the bombardment
(though before Bonaparte entered the town)
the thing—my masterpiece!—was stolen
from its case by old Countess Zacharoff
and later vanished in the deplorable
looting of the Zacharoff residence . . . .

from *Poetry*

The Necessary Angel

◊   ◊   ◊

What a simple lot we were, but she,
raspingly clever, kept us breathless,
our innocuous moxie cresting to order.

Did this hurt us or hinder?
We changed into humans less familiar
yet a bit smarter and smarting

from abrasions and humiliations.
Poor Thalia—could she ever
come to a golden end—an apple

of the moon—some wondered and still do.
But she was Hollywood!
And worth pursuing we thought and did.

Men? Men are walk-ons she said. We agreed.
Surely one like her plays every crowd.
But this was our theatrical—we,

the performers. It was unsurpassable.
She claimed she cut the tips from curly
eyelashes which never grew back.

She didn't need their extra fillip.
Were her legs a trifle too muscular?
Enough's enough, perfection was hers

and always will be in our thoughts,
her laughter descending from center
stage to our capitulated hearts.

from *River Styx*

Unholy Sonnets

◇   ◇   ◇

I

Hands folded to construct a church and steeple,
A roof of knuckles, outer walls of skin,
The thumbs as doors, the fingers bent within
To be revealed, wriggling, as "all the people,"
All eight of them, enmeshed, caught by surprise,
Turned upward blushing in the sudden light,
The nails like welders' masks, the fit so tight
Among them you can hear their half-choked cries
To be released, to be pried from this mess
They're soldered into somehow—they don't know.
But stuck now they are willing to confess,
If that will ease your grip and let them go,
Confess the terror they cannot withstand
Is being locked inside another hand.

II

After the praying, after the hymn-singing,
After the sermon's trenchant commentary
On the world's ills, which make ours secondary,
After communion, after the hand-wringing,
And after peace descends upon us, bringing
Our eyes up to regard the sanctuary
And how the light swords through it, and how, scary
In their sheer numbers, motes of dust ride, clinging—

There is, as doctors say about some pain,
Discomfort knowing that despite your prayers,
Your listening and rejoicing, your small part
In this communal stab at coming clean,
There is one stubborn remnant of your cares
Intact. There is still murder in your heart.

III

Two forces rule the universe of breath
And one is gravity and one is light.
And does their jurisdiction include death?
Does nothingness exist in its own right?
It's hard to say, lying awake at night,
Full of an inner weight, a glaring dread,
And feeling that Simone Weil must be right.
Two forces rule the universe, she said,
And they are light and gravity. And dead,
She knows, as you and I do not, if death
Is also ruled or if it rules instead,
And if it matters, after your last breath.
But she said truth is on the side of death
And thought God's grace filled emptiness, like breath.

IV

Time to admit my altar is a desk.
Time to confess the cross I bear a pen.
My soul, a little like a compact disc,
Slides into place, a laser plays upon
Its surface, and a sentimental mist,
Freaked with the colors of church window glass,
Rides down a shaft of light that smells of must
As music adds a layer of high gloss.
Time to say plainly when I am alone
And waiting for the coming of the ghost

Whose flame-tongue like a blow torch, sharp and lean,
Writes things that no one ever could have guessed,
I give in to my habit and my vice
And speak as soon as I can find a voice.

from *The New Criterion*

ALICE JONES

The Foot

◇   ◇   ◇

Our improbable support, erected
on the osseous architecture
of the calcaneus, talus, cuboid,
navicular, cuneiforms, metatarsals,
phalanges, a plethora of hinges,

all strung together by gliding
tendons, covered by the pearly
plantar fascia, then fat-padded
to form the sole, humble surface
of our contact with earth.

Here the body's broadest tendon
anchors the heel's fleshy base,
the finely wrinkled skin stretches
forward across the capillaried arch,
to the ball, a balance point.

A wide web of flexor tendons
and branched veins maps the dorsum,
fades into the stub-laden bone
splay, the stuffed sausage sacks
of toes, each with a tuft

of proximal hairs to introduce
the distal nail, whose useless
curve remembers an ancestor,
the vanished creature's wild
and necessary claw.

from *ZYZZYVA*

Contempt

◇　◇　◇

"Lizards," he'd say, dispensing with local men, and then resheath
      his pen and huff back to his drafting table,
A fiber board pristined with vinyl and overhung with the ambiguous,
      linked appendages of maybe a dozen modular lights,
One of which, now, by some unfathomable kink of logic, he'd bring
      screeching down above
His latest renderings of nunlike, mestiza hens I'd named like missiles:
      the Star 5000, the T-100 Egg Machine.

Those days of fruitless scratching on a pad, those nights of Klee and
      Rilke, and what abortifacient labor
Leaves, instead of money, that sense of energy troweled out and
      slapped up, no more than a phrase or two
That sticks, a sketch, no novel, no painting, only time whining
      irrevocably and the feeling
Of events put off or missed: openings, autograph parties—What else?

The grudging knowledge that, even in this, we were lucky: recession
      was on; Vietnam still shipped its dead.
I had the job because a friend knew a friend; he was someone's son:
      a cardiologist or an architect—I never learned.
Except for the boss, Devon, a transplanted Englishman with waxed
      mustache who chain-smoked Virginia Slims and despised
      Americans,
And Gwendolyn, his Phi Beta Kappa secretary, we worked alone in
      a kind of paneled coop they'd rigged

Above a shop that printed invitations and sold used office machines,
      or we'd go out as a team—
Cullman, Springdale, Gainesville—on this particular morning on a
      road just dusted with the season's first snow,
Stravinsky on the stereo, the piney Georgia hills, our usual patter,
      high culture, high art,
And then the building, massive, white, impregnable, our destination
      then, where we'd come to make something,

One of those brochures or tracts that aspire, through much lyrical
      glut and bedazzlement of facts,
To be taken as an article, objective, empirical: four thousand *bons mots*
      of cant replete with scale drawings
And headed "The World's First Totally Integrated Poultry Processing
      Plant." Was that art? Is this?
Embellished in four colors, translated into Dutch, Spanish, and
      Portuguese? That moment when he said it, "Lizards"?

Or later, when the door opened and the stench of bowels, lungs, and
      hearts welled up to us from the line
That we could just now make out through the steam, that first
      denuded glimpse of carcasses shedding slaughter
And strung by the talons as they moved through the faceless maze
      of women as in some gothic laundry
Fellini might have drudged up for the illuminati in heartfelt homage
      to the enduring spirit of Soutine.

Just that moment then, before a big man, someone officious, a plant
      manager or engineer, herded us in,
A handshake, a nod, and saying, "Here, take these," he gave us each
      a bag marked "Sanitation Suit,"
The silly bag-boy hats, paper coats, and thin latex gloves that now
      we had to haul on as he led us
Through the machines—the stunner, the killer, the plucker, the
      eviscerator, the de-lunger, the stripper, the chiller—

Each with its grisly attendant, those women, those Picassoesque
      smocks bespattered with yellow and red,
That proletariat chorus line, winking, emoting cool or hard-to-get,
      pregnant high school dropouts,

Tattooed grandmothers, chubby peroxide blondes wagging their
    fannies for the wheels.
So I knew, before the word had formed in the brain, before my
    friend had covered his lips with one hand,

And said it in that whisper that frames the sneer and gives it a secret
    eloquence, that it was coming,
Like one drop melting from a high icicle, falling, and spitting against
    a rock, "Lizards"—
And then, though how could any have heard, those women, as
    though in antiphony—what is the word?—words?—
"Sang," "jeered," "hooted," "whistled," "booed," "crowed,"
    "honked," "squawked"?

If you had ever heard five hundred North Georgia women in
    full-throated glory, parodying the morning cacophony of
    a barnyard
And knew that sound was meant for you, you would know how
    God sometimes
Will call a brother out of the terrible fields, and why the rest of that
    day stands out on the map of days,
Even the Chicken Teriyaki they served at lunch, and the ride back,
    snow skunking the ridges—our big idea

To name one bird and follow it from the chicken house through the
    plant, but gently, describing the genius
Of each machine, and on to the grocery store, where, yes, that was
    it, a young housewife, no, a widow would pick it up,
Bells would ring, a handsome man, the president of the company,
    we'd say, would step out from behind the frozen dinners,
And present a check, ten thousand dollars, and then—dissolve to
    dinner—*an idea of tenderness*, we'd call it,

But would it fly? Each day, I'd write, he'd draw. "Lizards," he'd say
    by way of greeting and goodbye.
Each night at the strip-bar in the shopping center, we'd drink on it.
    "Rilke is greater than Keats."
"Warhol follows naturally from Mondrian, but what I'm after in my
    work—call it Caravaggio with a gun—

Is riskier, everything exposed between the observation and display";
      then, "Imagine what it means,

Living in a place like this, loving men—Men?—Reptiles, lizards,
      slopes!"—
We'd see them crawling from the bathroom to the stools, and then
      the women would mount them,
Shut their eyes, and grind down hard in that mockery of a dance
      they do that seems at first
A quote of love's best motions, then just work, then the promise
      withdrawn, gone, the money and the girl—

Some guys would shrug and grin; others bluster up, throats
      tightening, fists purpling above the watered gin,
Before the rage guttered in an epithet of joke they'd still be slurring
      as they stumbled out into the cold.
Some nights we'd stay until the place grew quiet, late, and later,
      a fierce clinking of bottles; now light
Above the steel mills; now voices: dogs, birds. What would become
      of us?

from *Michigan Quarterly Review*

Courting the Famous Figures at the Grotto of Improbable Thought

◇ ◇ ◇

A jester or a buffoon might play with demons and not pay.
A jester might see these vines as bell ropes
And drag a sound from them. A commiserating sound. Rain
Or bird fall through wet air. The fall of angels.

God watched the angels fall. It was something like
A thunderstorm: out of keeping with the season: spectacular
In the way it dressed the sky: a surge of romantic music
Overplayed: and then that feeling of famous entry.

A jester might deliver a benediction but who would believe him?
Would God? Would God in his sad figure here? Would you?
The statue is very cold. It is lodged in the cave
Like a pocket mirror reflecting our distress. The boy

Lies dead on his mother's legs: his arm dropped:
Like the head of a flower dropped: the stalk snapped:
The head trailing: the mother's face afflicted
With the indecency of it all: the undressed moment:

The exposure of the broken motion. The statue might have been
A lamp if the stage had been managed properly. But
The double figure is only a shrunken reproduction: one
Of a thousand rabbit-like offspring of a more solemn notion.

The original that the madman leapt over the velvet ropes
To disfigure with his busy hammer keeps lurking
Behind it and laughing. Or is that the madman laughing?
There are no ropes here. The boy is lost to the wet shades.

He sleeps a child's sleep: his face bearded by the milk
He drank before bed: the milk beard: the beard before the man
Beard that these walls have grown. They have grown a face.
Not like the face of Moses who broke the tablets of the law.

Not like splendid Moses who came down from the mountain
And burned the golden calf to powder. And made the sons
Of Israel drink it. A magnificent rebuke. A meal
Of such extravagance it had to be concocted from phantoms.

But more like the face of a bearded lady: vaguely indecent:
Sexual in its longing. Water braids down the swollen vines.
And the moss is thick and singular: frosted with pale
Fluorescence. The story seems to be about overblown failure.

A passion for the morose. For perpetual rains. A heavy
Foot on the pedal prolonging the melancholic denouement.
The candles quaver in the long shadows the pines lay down.
And the saints assume their assigned postures: Posture

Of swallowing the ribald joke whole. Posture of turning
The quiet cheek for yet another slung tomato or stone.
One saint pulls his plaster cassock up with a coy motion,
His perfect lips pouted, exposing for us the leg wound

That was healed: a figure of the sweet lyric. Tra la la la.
Because it worked out wisely. Because it worked out well.
At his naked feet the sparrows scatter seed on the wet
Pavement. The child who sells holy trinkets feeds them. . . .

Now, see. We came for a revelation. A thick-headed
Generation: needing a miracle. We came for a show of Mercy.
Something as tangible as the trees' dropped cones: full
Of like kind: of like seed. Something we could juggle

Or plant against the coming need. We came with our orders
In hand. We came with our costumes. We had practiced
Our roles for a long time: the songs of suffering heroically
Endured, the parables and puns, conundrums and complaints,

The pantomimed fables and two-headed jokes, limericks and jigs,
The whole bag of tricks designed to catch God off guard
And relieve him of one or two of his multitudinous gifts.
We followed the rules. Though your ankles are weak

We climbed the steep cliff to the main attraction. The Goliath
The grotto is named for: The Lady of Improbable Thought.
The Lady of Prolonged Silence. The Lady of Strange Shape
That the hand of Anonymous hammered from the stone.

High-wrought hand. Awkward but unique. Possessing the power
Of origins. How many years did it contend with the Lady?
How many hammer blows to uncover the brow? The neck?
The giant cloaked breasts that paraded above us?

The Lady is a ship stalled and willing for the wait.
The gulls cut from her skirt cross over. She is ship
And figurehead in one: a blind form: having no pupils.
(Unless we are her pupils? The sight she has forsaken?)

We followed the rules. *We followed them all.* We moved
About her skirts: the blank tablets of her nomenclature:
We skirted the main issue. We did our tricks
And waited for applause. Was that it in the bird flurry?

Was that it in the yellow rag trussed to the tree?
Water dripped down the stone. There was the smell of dirt
And the smell of small illegal fires. There was
Expectancy and need: the clearing they made in the trees

Through which something might have moved. But
There was a deficit in the faculty of the Imagination.
We were no lions of Judah. We had no slingshot.
Not one smooth stone with which to reach her monstrous

Forehead. Wherever we stood the Lady looked away:
As if she were listening to something that made no sound:
Her sidewards habit shouldered by the art we've lost:
The assumption of the scene behind the scene: that pulls

The action forward: that gives it meaning. Couple
Vengeance with those things we cannot subtract. Coins
In the saints' cups. Smiles like weak flowers. Solace
Sliding as we did back down to this plaster strong-

Hold of saints. . . . *O Lady. O Lady. Around us an ocean.*
A field of disinterest. But still we push forward.
We bow, we bend. We keep moving. *Though we feel nothing.*
We keep moving. Here in the theater of public longing.

from *Northwest Review*

A Rune

◇　◇　◇

As I in *baden-zuyt* was entreating stop-and-go Pushkin here
around the dubious greensward (Hopkins, Brockles & Chippy *in
articulo mortis*), was I ever bonkers from the experience. *Bons coeurs*
I was. Took place entirely in the sack of sphagnum. Took place on
the slats with clone of Inigo Jones. Ottonian bricklayers "forgot"
how to lay brick. You might take one of them for a Lally column,
and I will Charleston with him (watch it that you do not sideswipe
the Briggs-Copeland incumbent). Then grrr, he picks up a Hamill
Wedge and where does that leave me? The HW is gravity flow, by
design. "Clean wet dog around house runs, indignant at bath";
loses weight in Amish Country, as against this.

And I was pronto and presto putting Quinquireme of Nineveh
and other prerequisites and emollients on the proper *complexioun*,
Nerd Mass at 5 PM (sensitive pastoral—even the priest is a nerd),
oyster stew 6, and then pool (and pool poem) at .004 knots. Got
lifeguard, Chris (not his real name) to do the math. Don some
laundry—"Lord Raglan." Hopkins, Brockles & Chippy validates
Lyon, Fish & Swan. Pushkin chomps the blefescue.

I write you parenting anyhow from Rhode Island and Providence
Plantations, which is patently half as you know under water; and
what *I* want to know is, there's a chop in the fingerbowl (pathetic
fallacy), why don't they move the Indy to the Astrodome? Will

you guys please row the damned Grand Rapids boat ashore? Making orphic-type music out of dead pieces of tree and old tusks: Sigmund Romberg. So please burn this now, OK?

from *Fine Madness*

KENNETH KOCH

One Train May Hide Another

◇　◇　◇

(sign at a railroad crossing in Kenya)

In a poem, one line may hide another line,
As at a crossing, one train may hide another train.
That is, if you are waiting to cross
The tracks, wait to do it for one moment at
Least after the first train is gone. And so when you read
Wait until you have read the next line—
Then it is safe to go on reading.
In a family one sister may conceal another,
So, when you are courting, it's best to have them all in view
Otherwise in coming to find one you may love another.
One father or one brother may hide the man,
If you are a woman, whom you have been waiting to love.
So always standing in front of something the other
As words stand in front of objects, feelings, and ideas.
One wish may hide another. And one person's reputation may hide
The reputation of another. One dog may conceal another
On a lawn, so if you escape the first one you're not necessarily safe;
One lilac may hide another and then a lot of lilacs and on the Appia
　　　　Antica one tomb
May hide a number of other tombs. In love, one reproach may hide
　　　　another,
One small complaint may hide a great one.
One injustice may hide another—one Colonial may hide another,
One blaring red uniform another, and another, a whole column. One
　　　　bath may hide another bath
As when, after bathing, one walks out into the rain
One idea may hide another: Life is simple

Hide Life is incredibly complex, as in the prose of Gertrude Stein
One sentence hides another and is another as well. And in the
     laboratory
One invention may hide another invention,
One evening may hide another, one shadow, a nest of shadows.
One dark red, or one blue, or one purple—this is a painting
By someone after Matisse. One waits at the tracks until they pass,
These hidden doubles or, sometimes, likenesses. One identical twin
May hide the other. And there may be even more in there! The
     obstetrician
Gazes at the Valley of the Var. We used to live there, my wife and I,
     but
One life hid another life. And now she is gone and I am here.
A vivacious mother hides a gawky daughter. The daughter hides
Her own vivacious daughter in turn. They are in
A railway station and the daughter is holding a bag
Bigger than her mother's bag and successfully hides it.
In offering to pick up the daughter's bag one finds oneself confronted
     by the mother's
And has to carry that one, too. So one hitchhiker
May deliberately hide another and one cup of coffee
Another, too, until one is over-excited. One love may hide another
     love or the same love
As when "I love you" suddenly rings false and one discovers
The better love lingering behind, as when "I'm full of doubts"
Hides "I'm certain about something and it is that"
And one dream may hide another as is well known, always, too. In
     the Garden of Eden
Adam and Eve may hide the real Adam and Eve.
Jerusalem may hide another Jerusalem.
When you come to something, stop to let it pass
So you can see what else is there. At home, no matter where,
Internal tracks pose dangers, too; one memory
Certainly hides another, that being what memory is all about,
The eternal reverse succession of contemplated entities. Reading
     A Sentimental Journey look around
When you have finished, for *Tristam Shandy*, to see
If it is standing there, it should be, stronger
And more profound and theretofore hidden as Santa Maria Maggiore

May be hidden by similar churches inside Rome. One sidewalk
May hide another, as when you're asleep there, and
One song hide another song: for example "Stardust"
Hide "What Have They Done to the Rain?" Or vice versa. A
        pounding upstairs
Hide the beating of drums. One friend may hide another, you sit at
        the foot of a tree
With one and when you get up to leave there is another
Whom you'd have preferred to talk to all along. One teacher,
One doctor, one ecstasy, one illness, one woman, one man
May hide another. Pause to let the first one pass.
You think, Now it is safe to cross and you are hit by the next one.
        It can be important
To have waited at least a moment to see what was already there.

from *The New York Review of Books*

DIONISIO D. MARTÍNEZ

Avant-Dernières Pensées

◊ ◊ ◊

IDYLLE

In today's mail I found the chain letter you've been sending for years. I know your handwriting, your desperation, the peculiar way in which you fold the paper. This plea, you tell me, has been around the world three, maybe four times. This plea is sacred. This plea is our last hope for anything. In theory, intimidation can penetrate anything. We all break sooner or later. The letters are carefully packed with case histories that go off like timed explosives. I can see you waiting for each one to go off, wondering if the one you designed for me will do the trick. One summer, you say, a Portuguese fisherman received this letter and burned it. He spent the rest of his life trying to read the ashes.

AUBADE

I thought it over. This letter is not sacred. It promises nothing. It is a plea for anything, which is like saying a plea for nothing. There was a faint barking as I walked toward the window. It was the sound dogs make when a stranger approaches. I began to doubt my own presence in the house, my hands opening the window to more barking. You must copy the entire letter, you said. The copies you make, the warning continued, must be indistinguishable from the source. I made the copies. I slept with the words beside me. This morning I thought it over. I tore the letter, replaced it with a blank sheet, folded the sheet in that peculiar way I learned from you.

MÉDITATION

On the coast of Portugal they began a tradition, you say. With the letters still inside the sealed envelopes, the wives of fishermen burn the mail they receive. This way, you tell me, superstition is impossible. But isn't this a superstition of sorts? It's really a mockery of belief, you say. I sometimes wonder how we've managed to correspond this long through chain letters. I wonder how we've been able to sustain this dialogue between two anonymous voices. I think of the widows along the Portuguese coast, their chain mail used as fuel for their stoves. I think of them selling rotten cod fish wrapped in anonymous letters that have circled the world three, maybe four times. I am spending the night in Viana do Castelo. I will send this postcard unsigned.

from *Seneca Review*

J. D. McCLATCHY

Found Parable

◇ ◇ ◇

In the men's room at the office today
some wag has labelled the two stalls
     the *Erotic* and the *Political*.
The second seems suitable for the results
of my business, not for what thinking
     ordinarily accompanies it.
So I've locked myself into the first because,
though farther from the light bulb overhead,
     it remains the more conventional
and thereby illuminating choice.
The wit on its walls is more desperate.
     As if I had written them
there myself, but only because by now
I have seen them day after day,
     I know each boast, each plea,
the runty widower's resentments,
the phone number for good head.
     Today's fresh drawing:
a woman's torso, neck to outflung knees,
with breasts like targets and at her crotch
     red felt-tip "hair" to guard
a treasure half wound, half wisecrack.
The first critic of desire is always
     the self-possessed sensualist.
With all that wall as his margin,
he had sniffed in smug ballpoint
     OBVIOUSLY DONE BY SOMEONE
WHO HAS NEVER SEEN THE REAL THING.

Under that, in a later hand,
    the local pinstripe aesthete
had dismissed the daydreamer's crudity
and its critic's edgy literalism.
    His block letters had squared,
not sloping, shoulders: NO,
BY SOMEONE WHO JUST CAN'T DRAW.
    Were the two opinions
converging on the same moral point?
That a good drawing *is* the real thing?
    Or that the real thing
can be truly seen only through another's
eyes? But now that I trace it through
    other jokes and members,
the bottom line leads to a higher inch
of free space on the partition—
    a perch above the loose
remarks, like the pimp's doorway
or the Zen master's cliff-face ledge.
    THERE ARE NO REAL THINGS
writes the philosopher. But he, too,
has been misled by everything
    the mind makes of a body.
When the torso is fleshed out
and turns over in the artist's bed,
    when the sensualist sobs over her,
when the critic buttons his pants,
when the philosopher's scorn sinks back
    from a gratified ecstasy,
then it will be clear to each
in his own way. There is nothing
    we cannot possibly not know.

from *The New Yorker*

Following Her to Sleep

◇　◇　◇

My friend wears boots to sleep
so that I might learn her path.
I know the way now.

The room is as silent as a child in a closet.

I hang this notion from an instrument of hindsight
where it rocks at the appropriate moment like fortune's
cube on a string.

My neighbor with no arms wanted to know how it feels
to let something go.

I will need more than this map to get to sleep.

I tend the jonquils emerging from the volcanic
soil of her scalp.

A wave repeats itself in a bird cage.

I pay an elderly man to sit in a booth
and keep track of what crosses my mind:
a wedding where the only guests are former lovers
arranged by breast and penis size,
a doctor committing an emergency,
the echo of a silent *e*,
a plane always on the verge of landing.

Morale is down in the boneless,
lactic fist of my genitals.

I cut my fingernails and glue them inside a diary
under the heading: definitive text.

Once, I slept like a staircase in an abandoned home.
Now, the shape of the body and the body
compete for the same seat.

Make each person's nose the size of their ignorance.

I am irresponsible I lose the stars off my flag
which is invalid.

Turn on the lights and go to bed!

Check the bags under my eyes for explosives.

I sleep in separate beds.

from *Ploughshares*

Spike Logic

◇　◇　◇

Since my smeared blood has registered *beep beep beep*
a half-decent 166, I download 34 units of Regular Humulin, 52 units
of Lente (S166 ⊂ 34R + 52L / 900 calories and 45 minutes
of Stairmaster) then snap my cocked index fingernail to dropkick

sideways from the top of the syringe the stubborn little bubble
that otherwise might, Allah forbid, introduce a fatal embolism
into my maculate cardiovascular system. Dr. Michael Halle,
my most recent endocrinologist, he of the grizzled jaw and wheels

of fire flaming round his eyes, has been on my case hard
for the past several weeks to go from two to *shit* three
shots a day, this to all the more tightly control my sugar
levels, and as soon as *I don't find this stuff amusing anymore*

I stop mumbling and humming and cackling viciously *hyeah* to
　　　　myself
about how I never did anything, I never did *anything*, that caused me
to get diabetes, how I'd like to add *that* to the hemisphere's
burgeoning reservoir of ribbonworthy causes and T-shirtiana . . .

just as the perfectly ripe, six-percent-brown-splotches Chiquita
I'll anally slice into uniform three-eighths-inch-deep cylinders
for subsequent layered dispersal amongst 1 oz. Wheati and Equal
reminds me all over again I'm not quite intact and *I want to be perfect*
　　　　but so

could certainly have done without having to prick *just don't let me*
get started my fingertip before insulating my blood this warm morning
and evening and every last morning and evening and pretty soon
        morning
noon and night, especially now that my faux Proustian, already
        sizzling brain

is retrieving with hypermnemonic precision and velocity voices and
        mugshots
of persons convinced they've got health problems the minute they
        come down with liverspots,
strep throat, insomnia, root-canal-caliber cavities,
gingivitis (another advantage of having diabetes:

you don't have to floss), ulcers, acne, the wrong-sized cotton ball
for applying fresh witch hazel, nearsightedness, migraine, one testicle,
torn anterior cruciate or ulnar collateral ligaments, corns, ague,
distemper, alcohol or narcotic dependency, gas, cellulitis,

fractured tibia, psoriasis, hairiness, hairlessness, old
skin and bones, folks who will genially curse
as they recount, mucus-voiced, the history of their cold . . .
Because *our sickness must grow worse*

Because I do not want
Because I don't have my health
Because I don't want to have to be fitted, sweet ladies, for none
a these big-time wowzer breakthrough prostheses, have krypton

lasers focused on the backs of my eyeballs to cauterize capillaries
in order to inhibit, though not to reverse, retinopathy. Because I do
        not want
my kidneys to deteriorate to the point where I need my blood
        cleansed by
dialysis, assuming I meet my then HMO's criteria, assuming I have
        one, assuming

my fucked circulation hasn't crunched my nerves' capacity
to produce nitric oxide so I can't even fill out the HMO's *forms*, see,
        get a

1 2 1

hardon, track the moist grain of a nipple or gnawed pen or vulva.
Because as the blond guy from Shrimp Boat has lazily drawled, *I
     wasn't feeling*

that fine. On, literally, the other hand, the first president ever I *walking
pre-existing condition that I am* voted for has signed an executive order
making it legal again to use fetal tissue in research enhancing
the possibility of implanting functional, way less rejectionprone

islets of Langerhans into my gall bladder, kidney or liver. Wherever.
     Because
I want to be cured of this thing as of Monday. Because I want
to have never had it. Because
I do not want

Because what part of this last do you not understand, Dr. Mike
and Camillo Ricordi and colleagues at research facilities in Tokyo,
Rochester, Pittsburgh, Dublin, St. Louis, Los Angeles *yo!?*
as I stab my left thigh with the hollow and glistening spike.

from *Salmagundi*

JAMES MERRILL

Family Week at Oracle Ranch

◊ ◊ ◊

1. THE BROCHURE

The world outstrips us. In my day,
Had such a place existed,
It would have been advertised with photographs
Of doctors—silver hair, pince-nez—

Above detailed credentials,
Not this wide-angle moonscape, lawns and pool,
Patients sharing pain like fudge from home—
As if these were the essentials,

As if a month at what it invites us to think
Is little more than a fat farm for Anorexics,
Substance Abusers, Love & Relationship Addicts
Could help *you*, light of my life, when even your shrink . . .

The message, then? That costly folderol,
Underwear made to order in Vienna—
Who needs it! Let the soul hang out
At Benetton—stone-washed, one size fits all.

2. INSTEAD OF COMPLEXES

Simplicities. Just seven words—AFRAID,
HURT, LONELY, etc.—to say it with.
Shades of the first watercolor box
(I "felt blue," I "saw red").

Also some tips on brushwork. Not to say
"Your silence hurt me,"
Rather, "When you said nothing I felt hurt."
No blame, that way.

Dysfunctionals like us fail to distinguish
Between the two modes at first.
While the connoisseur of feeling throws up his hands:
Used to depicting personal anguish

With a full palette—hues, oils, glazes, thinner—
He stares into these withered wells and feels,
Well . . . SAD and ANGRY? Future lavender!
An infant Monet blinks beneath his skin.

3. THE COUNSELLORS

They're in recovery, too, and tell us from what,
And that's as far as it goes.
Like the sun-priests' in *The Magic Flute*
Their ritualized responses serve the plot.

Ken, for example, blond brows knitted: "When
James told the group he worried about dying
Without his lover beside him, I felt SAD."
Thank you for sharing, Ken,

I keep from saying; it would come out snide.
Better to view them as deadpan panels
Storing up sunlight for the woebegone,
Prompting from us lines electrified

By buried switches flipped (after how long!) . . .
But speak in private meanwhile? We may not
Until a voice within the temple lifts
Bans yet unfathomed into song.

4. GESTALT

Little Aileen is a gray plush bear
With button eyes and nose.
Perky in flowered smock and clean white collar,
She occupies the chair

Across from middle-aged Big Aileen, face hid
In hands and hands on knees.
Her sobs break. Wave upon wave, it's coming back.
The stepfather. What he did.

Little Aileen is her Inner Child
Who didn't . . . who didn't deserve . . .
Round Big Aileen, the horror kissed asleep,
Fairy-tale thorns grow wild.

SADNESS and GUILT entitle us to watch
The survivor compose herself,
Smoothing the flowered stuff, which has ridden up,
Over an innocent gray crotch.

5. EFFECTS OF EARLY "RELIGIOUS ABUSE"

The great recurrent "sinner" found
In Dostoyevski—twisted mouth,
Stormlit eyes—before whose irresistible
Unworthiness the pure in heart bow down . . .

Cockcrow. Back across the frozen Neva
To samovar and warm, untubercular bed,
Far from the dens of vodka, mucus and semen,
They dream. I woke, the fever

Dripping insight, a spring thaw.
You and the others, wrestling with your demons,
Christs of self-hatred, Livingstones of pain,
Had drawn the lightning. In a flash I saw

My future: medic at some Armageddon
Neither side wins. I burned with SHAME for the years
You'd spent among sufferings uncharted—
Not even my barren love to rest your head on.

6. THE PANIC

Except that Oracle has maps
Of all those badlands. Just now, when you lashed out,
"There's a lot of disease in this room!"
And we felt our faith in one another lapse,

Ken had us break the circle and repair
To "a safe place in the room." Faster than fish
We scattered—Randy ducking as from a sniper,
Aileen, wedged in a corner, cradling her bear.

You and I stood flanking the blackboard,
Words as usual between us,
But backs to the same wall, for solidarity.
This magical sureness of movement no doubt scored

Points for all concerned, yet the only
Child each had become trembled for you
Thundering forth into the corridors,
Decibels measuring how HURT, how LONELY—

7. TUNNEL VISION

New Age music. "Close your eyes now. You
Are standing," says the lecturer on Grief,
"At a tunnel's mouth. There's light at the end.
The walls, as you walk through,

Are hung with images: who you loved that year,
An island holiday, a high-school friend.
Younger and younger, step by step—
And suddenly you're here,

At home. Go in. It's your whole life ago."
A pink eye-level sun slants through the hall.
"Smell the smells. It's suppertime.
Go to the table." Tears have begun to flow

Unhindered down my face. Why?
Because nobody's there. The grownups? Shadows.
The meal? A mirror. Reflect upon it.
Before reëntering the tunnel say goodbye,

8. TIME RECAPTURED

Goodbye to childhood, that unhappy haven.
It's over, weep your fill. Let go
Of the dead dog, the lost toy. Practice grieving
At funerals—anybody's. Let go even

Of those first ninety seconds missed,
Fifty-three years ago, of a third-rate opera
Never revived since then. The GUILT you felt,
Adding it all the same to your master list!

Which is why, this last morning, when I switch
The FM on, halfway to Oracle,
And hear the announcer say
(Invisibly reweaving the dropped stitch),

"We bring you now the Overture
To Ambroise Thomas's seldom-heard 'Mignon,' "
Joy (word rusty with disuse)
Flashes up, undeserved and pure.

9. Leading the Blind

Is this *you*—smiling helplessly? Pinned to your chest
A sign: Confront Me If I Take Control.
Plus you must wear (till sundown) a black eyeshade.
All day you've been the littlest, the clumsiest.

We're seated face to face. Take off your mask,
Ken says. Now look into each other deeply. Speak,
As far as you can trust, the words of healing.
Your pardon for my own blindness I ask;

You mine, for all you hid from me. Two old
Crackpot hearts once more aswim with color,
Our Higher Power has but to dip his brush—
Lo and behold!

The group approves. The ban lifts. Let me guide you,
Helpless but voluble, into a dripping music.
The rainbow brightens with each step. Go on,
Take a peek. This once, no one will chide you.

10. The Desert Museum

—Or, as the fat, nearsighted kid ahead
Construes his ticket, "Wow, Dessert Museum!"
I leave tomorrow, so you get a pass.
Safer, both feel, instead

Of checking into the No-Tell Motel,
To check it out—our brave new dried-out world.
Exhibits: crystals that for aeons glinted
Before the wits did; fossil shells

From when this overlook lay safely drowned;
Whole spiny families repelled by sex,
Whom dying men have drunk from (Randy, frightened,
Hugging Little Randy, a red hound). . . .

At length behind a wall of glass, in shade,
The mountain lioness too indolent
To train them upon us unlids her gems
Set in the saddest face Love ever made.

11. THE TWOFOLD MESSAGE

(a) You are a brave and special person. (b)
There are far too many people in the world
For this to still matter for very long.
But (Ken goes on) since you obviously

Made the effort to attend Family Week,
We hope that we have shown you just how much
You have in common with everybody else.
Not to be "terminally unique"

Will be the consolation you take home.
Remember, Oracle is only the first step
Of your recovery. The rest is up to you
And the twelve-step program you become

Involved in. An amazing forty per cent
Of our graduates are still clean after two years.
The rest? Well . . . Given our society,
Sobriety is hard to implement.

12. AND IF . . .

And if it were all like the moon?
Full this evening, bewitchingly
Glowing in a dark not yet complete
Above the world, explicit rune

Of change. Change is the "feeling" that dilutes
Those seven others to uncertain washes
Of soot and silver, inks unknown in my kit.
Change sends out shoots

Of FEAR and LONELINESS; of GUILT, as well,
Toward the old, abandoned patterns;
Of joy eventually, and self-forgiveness—
Colors few of us brought to Oracle. . . .

And if the old patterns recur?
Ask how the co-dependent moon, another night,
Feels when the light drains wholly from her face.
Ask what that cold comfort means to her.

from *The New Yorker*

One of the Lives

◇   ◇   ◇

If I had not met the red-haired boy whose father
    had broken a leg parachuting into Provence
to join the resistance in the final stage of the war
    and so had been killed there as the Germans were moving north
out of Italy and if the friend who was with him
    as he was dying had not had an elder brother
who also died young quite differently in peacetime
    leaving two children one of them with bad health
who had been kept out of school for a whole year by an illness
    and if I had written anything else at the top
of the examination form where it said college
    of your choice or if the questions that day had been
put differently and if a young woman in Kittanning
    had not taught my father to drive at the age of twenty
so that he got the job with the pastor of the big church
    in Pittsburgh where my mother was working and if
my mother had not lost both parents when she was a child
    so that she had to go to her grandmother's in Pittsburgh
I would not have found myself on an iron cot
    with my head by the fireplace of a stone farmhouse
that had stood empty since some time before I was born
    I would not have travelled so far to lie shivering
with fever though I was wrapped in everything in the house
    nor have watched the unctuous doctor hold up his needle
at the window in the rain light of October

I would not have seen through the cracked pane the darkening
valley and the river sliding past the amber mountains
    nor have wakened hearing plums fall in the small hour
thinking I knew where I was as I heard them fall

from *The New York Review of Books*

I Was on a Golf Course the Day John Cage Died of a Stroke

◇ ◇ ◇

As in Frank O'Hara's best known poem, "The Day Lady Died,"
After much everyday foregrounding
A poet should perhaps discover
An "underground" celebrity's
Death through the media
But I search for little
          meaningful things,

Not exactly an appropriate tribute to John Cage.
Yesterday, the day John Cage had his
     stroke,
I saw Merce Cunningham wheeling
     his hip to hail a cab west
     on Broadway and 11th St.

I wonder if he was going to St. Vincent's Hospital.
Then this afternoon, about the
     time John Cage died, my friend
     Mae Fern and I were
     walking through the Staten Island Greenbelt.
     We lost our way and decided to
     find our car by hiking on a street
     alongside the nature preserve.

Mae Fern is from Arkansas and I
asked her about the presidential election.
  She said she grew up
  in Arkansas with Bill and Hillary
  always in the background
  but as somewhat
  peripheral figures.
It was funny to leave Arkansas
  and learn more about them
On a grander scale than
  ever seemed possible at home.
Hillary had spoken to her high school and
  she seemed "cold" and "mean" to her,
Yet she felt that the Clintons
  had done some good things
Such as set up the 11th grade
  exceptional students' art enhancement
Program. She said it was very "liberal,"
  and she cited John Cage as an example
  of the work they did. "John Cage
  was there?" I asked.
  "No, but we performed
  John Cage pieces like
  the one with about ten radios."
"Oh yeah, no one ever finds
  a radio station, right?" "Right."
I remember John Cage in 1977 in his Bank Street basement loft,
  before he moved to the Avenue of the Americas,
  (he called the basement space "Merce's nightclub"
  and said if he ever had a view
  he'd "drink it up") typing
  a one page poem for a one
  page poetry magazine that
  Ken Deifik and I were putting out then.
He told me about a Merce Cunningham
  piece to be performed at the Minskoff Theater
  which consisted of the excess parts
  of other pieces. I said
  I'd like to see it. He gave me a ticket

to a matinee. When I
got there I was sitting next to him.
"Did you hear that Carter
pardoned the draft resisters?"
I asked.
"Oh, you mean the boys in
Canada?" he replied.
I really wish I had showed
him more of my poetry.
I don't think I ever sent
him my book, *Art Is Boring
for the Same Reason We Stayed
in Vietnam.*
I never told him that
I didn't work as he did
based on an urge not to repeat
that he nourished—
I never told him I wanted to
deprogram chance.
Once we were walking to his
favorite West Village Xerox store
when he asked me which
poets had most influenced me.
I told him that he had
because he taught me
to try to write so as not to ruin "nothing."
"That's very hard," he said.
Once we were driving down
34th Street when it began to
get ominously dark.
"Sometimes one forgets that New
York is just a seaside
town," he said.

from *Poetry New York*

Allegory

◇ ◇ ◇

The cockatoo hears gamelan,
    and dances.
The peacock hears rude voices in his head.
The swallow hears her happiness
    caroming all around her;
the grackle hears his doom being sealed.
The blue jay hears the cardinal,
    his loyal opposition.
The seagull hears a sharp insoluble debate.
The vulture hears the fine world's
    vulgar gossip, notes it well;
ambitious robin keeps his shrewd ear low,
    and hears the dew

        vanish, the shade
        steal, the cat
        mouse, the grass
        cover the worm.
The crow hears lies, lies, lies, and cries
    out curses. Nighthawk hears the crow's
    lyrical soul.
The mockingbird hears comedy
    in all this.
The dove hears pain
    in all this.

The lesser bird of paradise
        hears, but can't sing.
The phoenix hears the sirens crying *fire!*,
        and dances.

from *Colorado Review*

From Muse & Drudge

◊ ◊ ◊

Fatten your animal for sacrifice, poet,
but keep your muse slender.
Callimachus

1.

sapphire's lyre styles
plucked eyebrows
bow lips and legs
whose lives are lonely too

my last nerve's lucid music
sure chewed up the juicy fruit
you must don't like my peaches
there's some left on the tree

you've had my thrills
a reefer a tub of gin
don't mess with me I'm evil
I'm in your sin

clipped bird eclipsed moon
soon no memory of you
no drive or desire survives
you flutter invisible still

another funky Sunday
stone-souled picnic
your heart beats me
as I lie naked on the grass

a name determined by other names
prescribed mediation
unblushingly on display
to one man or all

travelling Jane
no time to settle down
bee in her bonnet
her ants underpants

bittersweet and inescapable
hip signals like later
some handsome man kind on the eyes
a kind man looks good to me

3.

I dream a world
and then what
my soul is resting
but my feet are tired

half the night gone
I'm holding my own
some half forgotten tune
casual funk from a darker back room

handful of gimme
myself when I am real
how would you know
if you've never tasted

a ramble in brambles
the blacker more sweeter juicier
pores sweat into blackberry tangles
going back native natural country wild briers

4.

country clothes hung on her all and sundry
bolt of blue have mercy ink perfume
that snapping turtle pussy
won't let go until thunder comes

call me pessimistic
but I fall for sour pickles
sweets for the sweet
awrr reet peteet patootie

shadows crossed her face
distanced by the medium
riffing through it
too poor to pay attention

sepia bronze mahogany
say froggy jump salty
jelly in a vise
buttered up broke ice

5.

battered like her face
embrazened with ravage
the oxidizing of these
agonizingly worked surfaces

that other scene offstage
where by and for her he descends
a path through tangled sounds
he wants to make a song

blue gum pine barrens
loose booty muddy bosom
my all day contemplation
my midnight dream

something must need fixing
raise your window high
the carpenter's here
with hammer and nail

6.

sun goes on shining
while the debbil beats his wife
blues played lefthanded
topsy–turvy inside out

under the weather
down by the sea
a broke johnny walker
mister meaner

bigger than a big man
cirrus as a heart tack
more power than a loco motive
think your shit don't stink

edge against a wall
wearing your colors
soulfully worn out
stylishly distressed

from *Agni Review*

At the Lakehouse

◊ ◊ ◊

The man on the porch is only the man
    on the porch,
But the woman on the dock is also
    the woman in the water.

The woman trawls with a forked
    stick she found after a storm, she slags
Weeds water-heavy, thick, to free
    shoals for the minnows.

Once the man rowed her out
    to the rock, so she could pull up
A whole colony, and liberate
    the rock. The weed gets

    wound in chartreuse peaks.
After three days, the cones harden
    the man wheelbarrows them to the sleeping
Garden, to make the outline of the thing—

    the straw poking through the apertures,
He puts the lakeweed on the outlines of the body,
    two patient, would-be graves, stalwart, waiting
For the frost and then waiting again.

The lakeweed will bear
   down into the growing, the wire
Around the fence will keep
   the deer away, will keep

   the geese in the river,
Will keep the water from the land.
   Will it? The porch creaks
as the teenager across the lake

   abandons her book, and the rain
Starts. The screen door bangs on its
   hinges. The linden bends under
The wind, all the while the pull,

   and the woman on the porch, waiting.
The rain spatters the cove, beheads the ferns,
   the rain means stay put, remain.
The man puts letters in boxes with a pen,

   the woman watches the rowboat capsize,
The yellow canoe flips behind the rock.
   "Sow the wind and reap the whirlwind"
the woman's mother, my grandmother,

   said once. The book gets blown
Into the lake. Rain. Raining. Rained.
   Here a tree got pulled up, the roots
hang down in a bad beard, the child's

   guessing game comes back, fingers held
Up in the air. The gap underneath is a mouth
   full of water. The spindly grove's
Bereft of bright red fruit, the sky burnt blue

   the ground wet beside the burn.
The lakeweed's wet again,
   flattened by the pound. On the path
is the branch, the woman strips it to a stick—

she was my best aunt,
    her grey hair basted on her head,
Stuck-in-place. Bullied into sainthood
    by his meanness, her gentility,

    sentinel, lake-keeper, breaking
into wildness as the wind hits the surface
of the lake. But more seldom.
And too late.

from *Colorado Review*

FRED MURATORI

Sensible Qualities

◊   ◊   ◊

It took the sea to prove a magnitude agreed on,
and since those who ventured that far disagreed, slashed each
other's limbs when lies mismatched and one man's serpent
dwarfed another's, our sphere of argument contracts:
in fields on their hands and knees, grousing through
tall grasses meant to yellow undisturbed, empiricists
pack beetles into sample bags, counting legs, making notes
in shorthand. Lightning apprehension is the goal.
Prolonged examination changes things, they die and change,
the changed observer dies, death's meaning changes,
complexities accumulate for future offspring bred
to sort them out in minutes cleared between the gathering
of fuel and nourishment. Our legacy. The quantity
of known phenomena dwindles through forgetfulness to one
unbudging core, what sight obliges us to measure out.

from *No Roses Review*

The Knowing

◊   ◊   ◊

Afterwards, when we have slept, paradise-
comaed, and woken, we lie a long time
looking at each other.
I do not know what he sees, but I see
eyes of surpassing tenderness
and calm, a calm like the dignity
of matter. I love the open ocean
blue-gray-green of his iris, I love
the curve of it against the white,
that curve the sight of what has caused me
to come, when he's quite still, deep
inside me. I have never seen a curve
like that, except the earth from outer
space. I don't know where he got
his kindness without self-regard,
almost without self, and yet
he chose one woman, instead of the others.
By knowing him, I get to know
the purity of the animal
which mates for life. Sometimes he is slightly
smiling, but mostly he just gazes at me gazing,
his entire face lit. I love
to see it change if I cry—there is no worry,
no pity, a graver radiance. If we
are on our backs, side by side,
with our faces turned fully to face each other,
I can hear a tear from my lower eye
hit the sheet, as if it is an early day on earth,

and then the upper eye's tears
braid and sluice down through the lower eyebrow
like the invention of farming, irrigation, a non-nomadic people.
I am so lucky that I can know him.
This is the only way to know him.
I am the only one who knows him.
When I wake again, he is still looking at me,
as if he is eternal. For an hour
we wake and doze, and slowly I know
that though we are sated, though we are hardly
touching, this is the coming the other
brought us to the edge of—we are entering,
deeper and deeper, gaze by gaze,
this place beyond the other places,
beyond the body itself, we are making
love.

from *American Poetry Review*

Them

◇ ◇ ◇

"Only they know who is them."

Their momentum was the point of having
successfully dicked someone over.

abnormal forces frequently produce structural distortions
they left a trail of bits of string cloth tiny chunks of
foam as from a cushion   woodchips   & bark shreds as
though they were losing   their stuffing as they walked

Like great islands they left the table
slowly they would lift their arms in the draperies
exposed the moon made donuts on their shoes
they rather understated a close to the ground charm
nearer to speech than being white or egg-shaped
ignored by all the stand-up comics and flowers

but that was the first thing
later they left a trail of elements
their dress sometimes died   from   its effects.

from *Poetry New York*

Divided Touch, Divided Color

◇ ◇ ◇

—Georges Seurat

As soon as I walked out I felt the mistake in the weather,
how the lesser light on the droplets hanging and flying
off the yew's bough had fooled me into readiness
for a chill. It was a Tuesday. I'd made my note on the yew berries,
how beautifully distinct from green they are, even in minimal light.
What satisfying clusters! Seeing one, one seeks another
and the tree responds easily in particles nearly rational,
or rationally assigned: the range of blues grouped beneath a smaller
        range
of grays, and then one sees the tree. Forgive me. I hesitate to tell
how frightened my little walk made me. It was a Tuesday,
the day my father comes. I wore the scarf and gloves.
In the graveyard I feel calmer, but the oaks had been changed, opened,
emptied since the last time by one rain. I saw they had become a
        line of cries,
and felt them filling me before my mind could think. Then the crow
        flocks
circled and fell in, binding every opening along the topmost edge
in a shrieking charcoal line, a line trying to enclose a shape and failing,
making the eye curl around. Someone, thinking of snow, had placed
        a toy
on every child's grave. That night, Signac came for dinner,

shocked by father juggling the knives, one of which he screws into
      the false end
of his arm. In my plate I see a painting of a plate. In my wife,
a jar of powder. My father is a black line eating snow.

from *Colorado Review*

CARL PHILLIPS

A Mathematics of Breathing

◊   ◊   ◊

I

Think of any of several arched
colonnades to a cathedral,

how the arches
like fountains, say,

or certain limits in calculus,
when put to the graph-paper's cross-trees,

never quite meet any promised heaven,
instead at their vaulted heights

falling down to the abruptly ending
base of the next column,

smaller, the one smaller
past that, at last

dying, what is
called perspective.

This is the way buildings do it.

II

You have seen them, surely, busy paring
the world down to what it is mostly,

proverb: so many birds in a bush.
Suddenly they take off, and at first

it seems your particular hedge itself
has sighed deeply,

that the birds are what come,
though of course it is just the birds

leaving one space for others.
After they've gone, put your ear to the bush,

listen. There are three sides: the leaves'
releasing of something, your ear where it

finds it, and the air in between, to say
equals. There is maybe a fourth side,

not breathing.

III

In my version of the *Thousand and One Nights*,
there are only a thousand,

Scheherazade herself is the last one,
for the moment held back,

for a moment all the odds hang even.
The stories she tells she tells mostly

to win another night of watching the prince
drift into a deep sleeping beside her,

the chance to touch one more time
his limbs, going,

gone soft already with dreaming.
When she tells her own story,

Breathe in,
breathe out

is how it starts.

from *Agni Review*

Pornography

◇ ◇ ◇

I. First Couple

On his knees, his back to us: the pale honeydew melons of his
    bare buttocks, the shapely, muscular hemispheres—

    the voluptuous center.

His knees push into the worn plush of a velvet cushion
    on the floral Oriental beside her cot.

He twists sideways—*contraposto*—and bends to put his face
    into her crotch, between her limp legs,

        one hoisted by his right shoulder, the other—more
        like an arm—reaching around his back, her ankle
        resting on his naked hip.

        She's wearing shiny slippers with bows; he has on
        bedroom slippers and socks.

He's got a classic profile: straight nose, sharp chin.
    Cowlick. His hair tapers high on his neck,
    outlines his ear, in the current fashion;
                        her
    curly bob gives away the date (barely '20s).

His mouth grazes her private hair; lips apart, he
    keeps his tongue to himself.

He's serious: if he were wearing clothes, and she were something
with pipes, he'd be a plumber's assistant—inspecting,
studious, intent;
nothing erotic in his look, hardly
aroused at all (a little hard to tell, of course,
from behind).

Flat on her back, on the dark, fringed spread, gravity
flattening her breasts, she looks

uncomfortable, but not unhappy. Her eyes
check out the camera. Her lips are sealed, yet—

isn't there?—a trace of smile
playing around the edges . . .

She stretches out an arm to him, places her palm
flat on his head—guiding him so lightly, she

might be blessing him.

II. SECOND COUPLE: THE SAILOR AND HIS GIRL

They're hot, half-dressed (upper half only), and they
can't wait.

He sports a sailor's midi and a mariner's
beret (is that a mound of fishing nets
she's lying back on?)
He rests his naked knee
beside her ample thigh.

Her dress is long—Victorian and striped. If she hadn't
raised it to her chest, it would be hiding her
black knee-length stockings and black, mannish shoes.
(He's also wearing shoes. How did he get his
pants off?)

No underwear—
                            nothing fallen around her
                                                    ankles
        to keep her from spreading her legs.

Not quite supine, she strains forward to eye, and
        hold, his bold erection:
                            bat and hardballs—
        major league (his Fenway Frank; his juicy
        all-day-sucker).

He looks down hungrily at her hungry eyes
        and mouth—one hand pressed flush against
        his own naked thigh.
                            He slouches a little (not all of him is
        standing at attention), to make what she wants
        easier for her to reach.

But the photographer is sharp—he keeps his sharpest focus
        on what he's sure we want it on: all the

        fleshy folds, clefts, crevices—the no-longer-
        secret places—of her welcoming flesh.

He knows the costumes negate the spiritual burden
        (and freedom) of pure nakedness—
                                    put us *in*
        medias res (things happening, things about
        to happen); in

        on the guilty secret, complicit—one eye
        furtively glancing over a shoulder . . .

His models rivet their attention on each other (did he
        have to tell them?), so that we can be

        riveted too.

Of course, they're only posing—
        but despite the props and costumes, certain

        undeniable details
        suggest that it isn't—it

        can't be—all an act.

III. MÉNAGE À TROIS

It's the heavy one—the one with the little pot belly, sagging
        breasts, and double chin (practically all we can
        see of her face)—that he's kissing so passionately.

Yet his arms are around them both, he loves them both
        (and of course he couldn't kiss them
        both at the same time).

Naked except for (like them) shoes and stockings, and garters,
        he sits at the edge of an overstuffed easy chair,
        his knees spread wide,
                                his massive cock
        rising like the Leaning Tower from his gut.

        His chest and neck, calves and thighs, have an athlete's
        sculptured musculature:

        exercise keeps all his parts in shape.

Both women are on their knees. She—the heavy one on his
        left (*our* right)—pushes into him, her round belly
        against his knee, her plush, round bottom
        a luxurious counterweight.

        Her fingers clutch his engorged organ, hang
        on to it, almost to steady herself.

The other one is slimmer, prettier, she has a pretty
        mouth—a delicate movie-star face.

    She's almost crouching, practically sitting on her
    own high heels; her right hand tenderly envelops
    his testicles.
                Hard to tell if she's smiling
    up at his face or down at his genitals—probably
    both, in equal admiration, adoration, desire.

His own benign, blissed-out look is
        harder to read, his shadowy profile
        half-buried in the intense kiss.

There's something sweet, *humane*, about them all: not
        innocent—
                but nothing (well, almost nothing) hard,
        or hardened yet.

    Only the little they have on reminds us how
    openly this was intended to be obscene.

The composition itself is elegant—balanced, symmetrical:
        the sweeping curve of the pretty one's behind
        and back, flowing up and across the curve of the
        man's shoulders and neck,
                        then down again through the
        fuller arcs of the plump one's back and rump—

    a harmonious circle of arms: theirs behind his back
    supporting him; his around them—his hands resting
    on their shoulders; their hands meeting in his lap . . .

It's like some medieval *Descent from the Cross* or *Holy
        Burial*: the slumping Christ between two
        ministering Angels—
                        but inside out, inverted, a negative
        of the Passion. Passion here only—and nothing
        but—passion. Perhaps

not even passion.

This ancient post card: cracked; corners broken; edges
    frayed; worn and fragile

    from use.

    How many has it gratified; disappointed;
    hurt? In whose horny fingers has it

    been gripped (and did that hand
    know what the other was doing)?

Not innocent—

    but nothing about them
    hard, or hardened yet;

    not yet past taking pleasure
    in whatever pleasure they

    receive, or give.

from *The Paris Review*

Pol Pot

◊ ◊ ◊

Dawn. Leni Riefenstahl
And her cameras slowly inflate the immense Nuremberg Rally.
The Colorado looks up in awe at the Grand Canyon
It has made. Hitler.

European clouds. 1934. Empty
Thought-balloons high above Lascaux
Without a thought inside. The Führer
Is ice that's fire, physically small.

They all were. Stalin.
Trotsky's little glasses
Disappear behind a cloud
From which he won't emerge alive.

The small plane carrying
The Grail to Nuremberg got Wagnerian clouds
To fly through, enormous, enormous. Mine eyes have see the glory, it
Taxis to a stop. The cabin door swings open.

Leni schussed from motion pictures
To still photography after the war. From the Aryan ideal, climbed out
In Africa to shoot the wild shy people of Kau,
Small heads, tall, the most beautiful animals in the world.

Artistically mounted them into ideal
Riefenstahl. Riefenstahl! Riefenstahl! Riefenstahl! Really,
From blonds in black-and-white to blacks in color.
Now Pol Pot came to power.

Now in London Sylvia Plath
Nailed one foot to the floor;
And with the other walked
And walked and walked through the terrible blood.

from *American Poetry Review*

ALAN SHAPIRO

The Letter

◇　◇　◇

The letter said you had to speak to me.
Please, if you love me, Alan, hurry. Please.

I read it and reread it, running down
the big stone steps into the underground,

and every time, as in an anagram,
the letters rearranged themselves again

as new words cancelling the ones before:
Come or don't come I really couldn't care,

I never meant to hurt you like I did.
I never hurt you. There's nothing to forgive . . .

The letter virulent with changing moods,
now cross, now pleading, accusing and accused,

seemed to infect each place I hurried through:
the slippery concrete of the vestibule,

the long low tunnel, and the turnstiles where
nobody waited to collect my fare,

nobody on the platform either, far
and near no sound within that mineral air,

nothing around me but a fever of clues
of what it was you wanted me to do.

O mother, my Eurydice in reverse,
was it the white line I was meant to cross?

To hear within its Thou Shalt Not a "Shall"
and follow you into a lower hell?

The page went blank. Below me now I saw
barbed wire running where the third rail was,

and in the sharp script of its angry weaving,
suspended in the loops and snares, the playthings

of forgotten life, dismembered dolls,
the frayed tip of a rubber knife, a wheel,

the tiny shatterings of cups and saucers,
and other things worn back into mere matter,

their glitter indecipherable except
as the star burst of some brief interest,

the barbed discarded relics of a wanting
they all intensified by disappointing.

As if they could be words, and those words yours,
obscuring what they substituted for,

each leading to a darker one beyond
the bleak lights of the platform, I jumped down

and there at last among them crawled and read,
burning with comprehension as I bled.

The pain was good, the pain exhilarated,
the pain was understanding, now perfected.

Cauled in my own blood, mute and lame and free
of everything obstructing you from me,

I saw your face above me leaning down.
There's nothing here for you, you said, go home.

It's for your own good, child, believe me, and
I vanished, waking, as you turned around.

from *The Threepenny Review*

Courtesan

◊   ◊   ◊

The air grows thin. The men are less bewitched
of late, no longer appeased with flagrant
dessert set aflame, nor wowed by shellacked
tenacity of my coiffure. Tumid
and ruthless, they loosen the latitude
round their middles, visibly bored. Someone's
perfume, they sense, glided through here, fragrant
and vacant. I dull like silver. My jokes
mold. The little dinner party's carnage:
thick, residual soup puddled in low
bowls, pumice-rough edges of bread, sottish
remnants of rum-laced cake. Now the onset
of sweet, swift redwine headache, my face still
stiff where I fit my simper. The plaster
holds though cold aspic ungels and candles'
drip hardens to sculpture. In the sofa's
leather the dim imprints visitors leave—
buttocks and thigh—turn vaguely lurid. Sad
ghosts of my lashes on scented tissue:
delicate mascara moth wings. Life pools
in the shallows. Later, unlaced, what breathes
in slip and stocking feet. Left to settle
what rich, indecent cream resurfaces.

from *Chelsea*

Read Your Fate

◇　◇　◇

A world's disappearing.
Little street,
You were too narrow,
Too much in the shade already.

You had only one dog,
One lone child.
You hid your biggest mirror,
Your undressed lovers.

Someone carted them off
In an open truck.
They were still naked, travelling
On their sofa

Over a darkening plain,
Some unknown Kansas or Nebraska
With a storm brewing.
The woman opening a red umbrella

In the truck. The boy
And the dog running after them,
As if after a rooster
With its head chopped off.

from *The New Yorker*

W. D. SNODGRASS

Snow Songs

◇ ◇ ◇

i.

one. now another. one
more, some again; then done.
though others run
down your windshield, when
up ahead a sudden
swirl and squall comes on
like moths, mayflies in a swarm
against your lights, a storm
of small fry, seeds, unknown
species, populations. every one
particular and special; each one
melting, breaking, hurling on
into the blank black. soon,
never to be seen again.
most never seen.
all, gone.

ii.

First, the exhausted, brown
leaves, then the snow comes down
the way a year's change shakes
hairs loose or those dull flakes
littering your shoulder.
Soon, windier and colder

gusts—as confetti falls
on our sunstruck festivals,
then, flurrying wilder, thicker,
scatters like heavy ticker-
tape over the parade
route and the motorcade
of some departing hero.
Now, into a near-zero
visibility
where nothing can be
known sure of events,
what with the pervasive, dense
smother of shredded documents.

iii.

White out; white out; so
      that the landscape's ledger
         balances again.
On the hill, the white-tailed deer's
      remains are spirited
         away like laundered funds:
flesh, pelt and all
      the inner workings nibbled
         down, salted away inside
the general, unmentionable,
      unseen economy of the woods.
         Bones, like the broken branches,
soften, sink back down
      in ground that sent them
         out to reconnoiter.
Soon this whole, broad
      Stalingrad will be no more
         than scattered fading photographs,
just some aging soldiers'
      recollections till at last

all thought dies down to the
perfection of the blank page
and the lighted
screen that will flick off.

iv.

The leading colonists of summer,
Carriers of what we called progress,
Uplift, or flat success,
Have gone south taking their plunder.
All crucial witnesses

Are safely hushed-up underground
Or live on on the season's scraps.
Thick snow blots out the maps;
The woods, the air, the memory's found
Compromised by gaps.

We're left with dwindled and diminished
Hopes, left with those hangers-on
Too listless to get gone,
With long abandoned, half-finished
Plans, conclusions drawn.

v.

The horizon, a maternal flour sifter,
Sprinkled your landscape; light winds lifted
Powdered sugar in your bowl; the drifting
Snow, white tissue paper for your gifts.

Now, coke on glass, powder on pocked cheeks; foam
On lip, lake, contact points; abundant mold
On the peaches, bird dung on the civic stones;
Whitewash, whitewash over Holy Wisdom's dome.

vi.

Now snow lies level
    with the windowsills. Along
the thruway, traffic
    like fresh water flows
between banks ten feet
    above our heads. Still
it sifts down slow
    as infinite, small
skeletons of diatoms drift,
    settling through the salt seas,
falling only inches year
    by year, some 20,000 species,
geometric, crystalline, no
    two shells alike, covering
the sea's floor hundreds
    of feet deep. Now turn
the radio up louder; try to
    catch the local dialect.

vii.

8,000,000 *alleluias* or
lace paper valentines, these
bitsy webs and doilies—
such dear wee scallops
on each twig, a sweet
tiara for each flower. Oh,
vast crochet hooks of the
skies, God's bobbin mills,

tat us this day our peekaboo
bra and scanties; glamorize
the gamey soiled loins of
one more incontinent season;
fall, plastic popcorn, pack

and seal the year up, draw
this dull white coverlet
over the patient's eyes.

viii.

Leaving the snow
      bank, your boot leaves
         a fossil print—an
emptiness remains. Just so,
      across the field you've made
        a trail of absences.
      Still the snow
falls—as a clean sheet smooths
        your shape out of the bed
      you don't go back to.
        You are the missing
      tooth, the one place
at the table, lost
        wax from the casting—though,
      long as they last,
these chicken scratchings hold
        the voice unspoken on
      the finished page as under
        plaster hardening,
a fading face.

from The Kenyon Review

The Robed Heart

◊　◊　◊

They come in white livery bringing the sun,
the Robed Heart astride her white mount,
crowds lining the royal road in anticipation.
Ahead, the castle flying the new colors,
a queen's great labors come to an end.
A shout, and the cord is cut,
the crown placed upon my head.

And I am, Mother, I am!

from *The Iowa Review*

A. E. STALLINGS

Apollo Takes Charge of His Muses

◇　◇　◇

They sat there, nine women, much the same age,
The same poppy-red hair, and similar complexions
Freckling much the same in the summer glare,
The same bright eyes of green melting to blue
Melting to golden brown, they sat there,
Nine women, all of them very quiet, one,
Perhaps, was looking at her nails, one plaited
Her hair in narrow strands, one stared at a stone,
One let fall a mangled flower from her hands,
All nine of them very quiet, and the one who spoke
Said, softly,

"Of course he was very charming, and he smiled,
Introduced himself and said he'd heard good things,
Shook hands all round, greeted us by name,
Assured us it would all be much the same,
Explained his policies, his few minor suggestions
Which we would please observe. He looked forward
To working with us. Wouldn't it be fun? Happy
To answer any questions. Any questions? But
None of us spoke or raised her hand, and questions
There were none; what has poetry to do with reason
Or the sun?"

from *The Beloit Poetry Journal*

The Mysterious Maps

◊　◊　◊

I

There is a certain triviality in living here,
A lightness, a comic monotony that one tries
To undermine with shows of energy, a devotion

To the vagaries of desire, whereas over there
Is a seriousness, a stiff, inflexible gloom
That shrouds the disappearing soul, a weight

That shames our lightness. Just look
Across the river and you will discover
How unworthy you are as you describe what you see,

Which is bound by what is available.
On the other side, no one is looking this way.
They are committed to obstacles,

To the textures and levels of darkness,
To the tedious enactment of duration.
And they labor not for bread or love

But to perpetuate the balance between the past
And the future. They are the future as it
Extends itself, just as we are the past

Coming to terms with itself. Which is why
The napkins are pressed, and the cookies have come
On time, and why the glass of milk, looking so chic

In its whiteness, begs us to sip. None of this happens
Over there. Relief from anything is viewed
As timid, a sign of shallowness or worse.

II

Low shadows skim the earth, a few clouds bleed,
A couple of grazing cows carry the next world
On their backs, their hides the mysterious maps

Of the principal countries. Too bad the future
Is covered with flies, and sits in a pasture.
Here comes old age, dragging a tale of soft

Inconvenience, of golfing in Florida,
Of gumming bad food. These cows never stop chewing.
O love, how did we get here, so far from the coast

Of our friends, our nervous talkative friends,
Who are now reading in bed or watching TV
Because it is later there, and they must

Keep their minds off missing us, off whatever
Would happen were we to come back from our exile?
And the earth is almost dark, the crickets

Are clicking, the laundry is in the dryer,
The heat of the night is giving us new things
To wish for. Who cares if we were young once—

The young don't care, the old don't care,
So long as they are not left behind.

III

A long time has passed and yet it seems
Like yesterday, in the mid-most moment of summer,
When we felt the disappearance of sorrow,

And saw beyond the rough stone walls
The flesh of clouds, heavy with the scent
Of the southern desert, rise in a prodigal

Overflowing of mildness. It seems like yesterday
When we stood by the iron gate in the center
Of town while the pollen-filled breath

Of the wind drew the shadow of the clouds
Around us so that we could feel the force
Of our freedom while still the captives of dark.

And later when the rain fell and flooded the streets
And we heard the dripping on the porch and the wind
Rustling the leaves like paper—how to explain

Our happiness then, the particular way our voices
Erased all signs of the sorrow that had been,
Its violence, its terrible omens of the end?

from *The New Yorker*

Offering

◇   ◇   ◇

In the dream I am burning the rice.
I am cooking for God. I will clean
the house to please Him. So I wash the dishes
and it begins to burn. It is for luck.
Like rice pelting newlyweds,
raining down it is another veil,
or an offering that suggests
her first duty: to feed him.

Burning, it turns brown, the color
of my father, whom I never pleased.
Too late, I stand at his bed,
calling. He is swathed in twisted
sheets, a heavy mummy that will not
eat or cry. Will he sleep when
a tall stranger comes to murder me?
Will I die this fourth time, or the next?

When I run, it is as if underwater,
slow, sluggish as the swollen grains
rising out of the briny broth to fill
the pot, evicting the steam in low
shrieks like God's breath sucked back in.
Before I slip the black husk of sleep,

I complete the task. The rice chars,
crumbles to dust, to mix with
the salty water, to begin again.

from *Callaloo*

Sleeping with Boa

◇ ◇ ◇

I show her how to put her arms around me,
but she's much too small.
What's worse, she doesn't understand.
And
although she lies beside me, sticking
out her tongue, it's herself she licks.

She likes my stroking hand.
And
even lets me kiss.
But at my demand:
"Now, do it to me, like this,"
she backs off with a hiss.

What's in her little mind?
Jumping off the bed,
she shows me her behind,
but curls up on the rug instead.
I beg her to return. At first, she did,
then went and hid

under the covers. She's playing with my feet!
"Oh, Boa, come back. Be sweet,
Lie against me here where I'm nice and warm.
Settle down. Don't claw, don't bite.
Stay with me tonight."
Seeming to consent, she gives a little whine.

Her deep, deep pupils meet mine
with a look that holds a flood . . .
But not my brand.
Not at all.
And,
what's worse, she's much too small.

from *The Yale Review*

Modern Times

◇ ◇ ◇

I

In the Sangre de Cristos near Santa Fe
where we'd hitched in a gold Caddy luminously set
on cruise control with two LA dealers,
me driving one long night through Oklahoma,
the car's trunk filled with heroin, we found
out later, we waited for peyote's bitters
to explicate green light under the aspen's
leaves that rattled and flashed with uncertain vision,
below us a raptor floating in cold air.
I try our particular good, our need
tonight, you dead of AIDS twenty years later,
some unlovely part of us, maybe,
sheer cellophane or a cigarette's plastic filter,
still somewhere in that dirt's woozy dark.

II

You taught me all the good, hard words for sex
while we learned *cleave*'s double meaning
in the brick house on San Francisco Street
below the Plaza, where Santo Domingo jewelers
spread blankets of cheap turquoise and silver
all day, and at night came to the Canton Cafe
drunk, picking me up in my white uniform
after the Chinese cook had pinched my ass
as I carried a weighted tray of dishes, covered,

through the kitchen's swinging doors. Crazy,
they spun me on a Formica table-top.
Crazy, I had never lived beyond the rich suburbs'
humid poolside metaphysics
derived from afternoon's languorous habits.

III

Sometimes the habitual looks out good
and finds necessity only. As now,
when hardness exceeds my capacity
to lie. Your mother has just described you
to me as a beautiful corpse, your eyes half-closed,
she said, like Jesus. I see you clearly,
a distracted hand raked back through your hair,
sweet jesus, laughing.
The miraculous, yet again, has withheld
its intervention. Color drags the mountains here,
pocked by Kaposi's, shadowed in the sunset's
afterglow, above what tourist writers call
the most open hole in the world.

IV

Without you, who remembers me? I lack
gratitude's pure form, the one affliction
calls forth. The grey and red bracelets
placed on you by the hospital staff
would have slipped nearly to the elbow
on your thin arm, I've been told, bruised black
by injections. Your body, the instrument
you had once lived through in order to dance,
would have been pain as you lifted yourself
higher onto your pillows to take your breath,
a patch of white gauze across your heart
where the fever only dropped its silver mark
too late, your old jazz-bar pallor
turned reckless. The day you died, a south wind

V

blew flowers into my room. The floor
whitened with petals. I'm unsure if we have
the right to desire union with anyone.
When we do, distance enforces itself.
Remember those one-night stands that mattered?
Passion in a delighted arc achieved
entirely between the larger accidents
of loss? A whole phylogeny of gestures,
beginning with small kisses curved to the line
of cheek and collarbone, became the great kiss,
unresisting flesh on flesh, pulled tight
for just that time. That gorgeous indifference.
Such perfection transformed into friendship,
sometimes. It was nearly universal.

VI

What if I could bring you back, I at last
the only one you acknowledged loving?
What would we do now with one another?
Life, anyway, enacts its mouth-to-mouth,
has turned us to achieve its right angle
of thigh to hip, of hip to fragile breastbone,
of breast to neck to tearing eye. It's left
behind what it can't digest, what's here.
We always knew that laws can be broken
only carefully, we depend on them
so much. Who can I blame? You have been taken,
I think, by low-riders we saw one night
driving by, their overhead light on,
all of them gesticulating wildly.

VII

If that time were a page that bloomed in fire
blackening, then curling from its straight edge

down slopes smelling of walnut and juniper
to this place, a dry gash under my lamp,
and if now that same defaced slope
resembles vertical script, words hanging
upward from some spring's unremitting green,
and if I long for letters pulled somehow
through all varieties of light, despite
my pen falling as edges cleave apart
to reveal and to protect such a secret,
and if we have had only creatures
to fuck, their intermediary frailty,
then I grieve for you.

VIII

That is the miracle. We turned, exhausted,
from one another. The teenage trick
of inhaling smoke held in someone else's lungs,
then passed through a deep kiss into the throat,
either mine or yours, was not the sign
of what was to come, of what possession
comes to. The mountains sliding heavily
onto us, even they never taught us
that only death stays up to arm-wrestle
attachment, if it can keep awake.
The one organ of contact with existence
is love. It calls me backward to the next
morning's startled graveyard where we talked
between anthills and plastic flowers,
amid its tin crosses, our regardless bodies.

from *Boulevard*

Like a Scarf

◊   ◊   ◊

The directions to the lunatic asylum were confusing;
most likely they were the random associations
and confused ramblings of a lunatic.
We arrived three hours late for lunch
and the lunatics were stacked up on their shelves,
quite neatly, I might add, giving credit where credit is due.
The orderlies were clearly very orderly, and they
should receive all the credit that is their due.
When I asked one of the doctors for a corkscrew
he produced one without a moment's hesitation.
And it was a corkscrew of the finest craftsmanship,
very shiny and bright not unlike the doctor himself.
"We'll be conducting our picnic under the great oak
beginning in just a few minutes, and if you'd care
to join us we'd be most honored. However, I understand
you have your obligations and responsibilities,
and if you would prefer to simply visit with us
from time to time, between patients, our invitation
is nothing if not flexible. And, we shan't be the least slighted
or offended in any way if, due to your heavy load,
we are altogether deprived of the pleasure
of exchanging a few anecdotes, regarding the mentally ill,
deprived, diseased, the purely knavish, you in your bughouse,
if you'll pardon my vernacular, O yes, and we in our crackbrain
daily rounds, there are so many gone potty everywhere we roam,
not to mention in one's own home, dead moonstruck.
Well, well, indeed we would have many notes to compare
if you could find the time to join us after your injections."
My invitation was spoken in the evenest tones,

but midway through it I began to suspect I was addressing
an impostor. I returned his corkscrew in a non-threatening manner,
what, for instance, I asked myself, would a doctor, a doctor of the
        mind,
be doing with a corkscrew in his pocket?
This was a very sick man, one might even say dangerous.
I began moving away cautiously, never taking my eyes off of him.
His right eyelid was twitching guiltily, or at least anxiously,
and his smock flapping slightly in the wind.
Several members of our party were mingling with the nurses
down by the duck pond, and my grip on the situation
was loosening, the planks in my picnic platform were rotting.
I was thinking about the potato salad in an unstable environment.
A weeping spell was about to overtake me.
I was very close to howling and gnashing the gladioli.
I noticed the great calm of the clouds overhead.
And below, several nurses appeared to me in need of nursing.
The psychopaths were stirring from their naps,
I should say, their post-prandial slumbers.
They were lumbering through the pines like inordinately sad moose.
Who could eat liverwurst at a time like this?
But, then again, what's a picnic without pathos?
Lacking a way home, I adjusted the flap in my head and duck-walked
down to the pond and into the pond and began gliding
around in circles, quacking, quacking like a scarf.
Inside the belly of that image I began
recycling like a sorry whim, sincerest regrets
are always best.

from *Colorado Review*

PATRICIA TRAXLER

Death of a Distant In-law

◇ ◇ ◇

We watched the deaf-mute buried
in his largest silence. Earlier
in the relatives' chapel his family,
brought together there, nodded, smiled,
and whispered about jobs and kids and cars,
catching up, while through the curtain drawn
to hide our tears, the preacher celebrated
This Man's Simplicity. This man. I thought of
family gatherings through the years, this distant
in-law in a corner chair somewhere, watching
the silent movie of our stir. Sometimes
he moved his lips, touched his useless ears,
cajoling; large eyes looming like dark
closets not sorted through in years.
Now he lay like marble, big hands clasped
across his heart, and finally his eyes were closed,
beneath the lids that unnamed knowledge
stored and locked away.

from *Agni Review*

The Snake in the Garden Considers Daphne

◊ ◊ ◊

My less erotic god condemned
my taste for girls less classical
than you, the kind that can't resist
a dazzling advance or trees that stand
for love. Of course I understand
up there it seems to be all light
and prelapsarian elation—but bear
in mind your lower half that gropes
for water, the slender roots you spread
in secret to fascinate the rocks,
while sunlight pries apart your leaves
and flights of birds arouse the air
around you. If only I could run
a brazen hand along this wood
and feel your heart accelerate
beneath it, rising to your lips.
If only you could pick the whitest
petals from the holy orchard
where I patrol the crevices
and slink along my damned gut,
you could arrange them as you wished
and change the ending of our story.
But we're disarmed, and nothing changes

in our natural gardens—we cannot grasp
the word *hope*, which the ones we've tempted
find always at their fingertips.

from *The Paris Review*

My Talk with
an Elegant Man

◇   ◇   ◇

What's to tell?
I was born in a steel town
where steel is twenty years gone,
and I live in a car town
where the plants have shut.

"But only, perhaps, like day lilies, to open again,"
intoned the man in the cocked hat.

No, I don't think so. Where are you from, anyway?

"I? I come from elsewhere, from a contented region
that resembles Provence. You really must visit."

No, I don't think so. But thank you. Thank you.

from *The Bridge*

Putting in a Word

◇   ◇   ◇

What you call me, when you call
Me names, names me, as long as it's
Your calling, but the meaning
Is my choice, is what I change
The word into, by being more
Than it can show; by being
More than me, alone. I copy
Lots of other folks, including
You. We're all sort of married
To each other at various times
And passes of conversation or
In the street, or in the car, or
At night when everyone's asleep, and
Dreaming starts for certain,
Offering selves and solutions to us
Although we'll never resolve what
We dreamed about. I wave
A scarf, pale silk chiffon
With a print of Morse code.
It flies from tower or tree
Or the attic room or the Metro North car
Named "John Cheever," full of those
Who bounce between two cities,
Who wear rings, own houses, hire
Other people on salary, drink whiskey,
Watch TV. Why aren't they like us?
What do their scarves say?
You see their names could never

Be like ours, even if
There isn't any word for what
We are, in relation, say
To them. I don't own that scarf, in
Fact; I saw it in a box of things for
Fifty cents apiece down cellar in the
Wooden church in Craryville, and I told you
About it, and you said, "Who
Could live without it?" and now
As you see, I am still living with it,
Largely because I left it there,
And then when I returned it wasn't
There, another day. And if I don't
Live with you, I don't live without
You, either, ever; the
Words have changed me; not
The names, I mean, but just
The ways of saying things, your
Ways: I can't forget, some
I mimic consciously, some
Without my knowing what I'm doing.
It's always so nice to
Hear from you, even this way,
In my voice, with your
Inflections. It's as though
You were still alive, or I
Were still sixteen, or we
Still lived in the same city,
On the same block, or as though
We hadn't fallen out of the
Habit of calling now and then.
"Wishing you were here,
I croon a tune to myself: it's
Your tune; and so I fool my fool
Self into thinking you're around;
I hear you talking." This,
I think, this is what love is,
Always putting in a word where
Absence sets the dinner table;
Raps and thumps from everyone not

There possess our voices, and we're
Possessed by their strong styles or rhythms;
Almost as good as eyes holding
Eyes, to hold your way
Of saying hi or laughing, in my
Mouth the quickest moment, like
Kissing air this person you're
Missing breathes, or breathed
While breathing.
                    Open the window
above the bed, the door below
the staircase. Come, seances,
Sentences, spirits: psyche me up.

from *Boulevard*

The One

◇ ◇ ◇

To the long mill's shadow
and stink we shared
with drunks who pissed
on the heater of our common
john I go back.
To the bedroom I shared with my sister,
my bed squeezed
tight against the cool wall
so I could hold my body there
hot nights in the mill noise
until my legs stiffened
and I felt that hum.
In the corner of that room
is the word and the sound
of the belt.
My tall father
thin and muscled
from mill work,
his hair black thick and curly,
his jaw long and square like mine
and his smile
when he swung down on me
could not be resisted.
Through dark the belt
flashed across my back
though I knew he beat me
out of love
as when he finished

I knew to climb inside
the darkness of my arms.
I knew the world would stop
spinning uncontrollably
and the convulsions
stop rippling
and my mother
would come touch me
with such care
as if I were teetering
at the edge of the abyss
and lead me back into my life,
her fingers
whispering in my hair
that it would be alright,
and later still, after beer,
after the moon had risen
to its proper place
and the night
could allow some forgiveness
he calls me into his lap
and tells me I am the one.

from *American Poetry Review*

JOSHUA WEINER

Who They Were

◇ ◇ ◇

Thanksgiving day, no one yet thinks of him
as dead, his loneliness a new career
with which he seems preoccupied and proud.
Eyes tracing us at lunch, the cane he hates
still gripped while sitting, he's all quiet cheer,
a cartoon smile beneath a rheumy stare
absorbing family pomp and the pitch
of conversation teasing him like slang
he sometimes understood. He plays his brow
like a signal flag so we can see he's there.
Assured and brainy even now, he begins to speak
deliberate roping sentences that coil
off the spool of stories spinning in his head:
How Uncle Doc, a plumber struck by lightning,
took care of two Jew-haters on the subway
by slamming heads together in a brawling kiss,
then hauling them like beaten luggage curbside
and stealing their cigars;—or he sees himself
a boy in Russia prior to the coup,
holding his mother's keys as she is shot
for running guns to Lenin . . .

                                    Was it true
or merely true enough?

                        Desperate to snare
some history late in middle age, my mother,
prepared with tape machine, holds out the mike:
"Say it again, Dad, speak into the thing."
He laughs and shakes his head, sips once and sighs,

the heaving past calm now beneath the surface
of everything he'd like to say, and shy
before posterity's cool instruments.

*

Another year, a stroke, yet still he is here;
speaks less; sings opera when the pizza comes.
He smiles at his son and recognizes me
but not my name or who I am: *grandson*:
a future pale as the once prized heirlooms
cramping his apartment, and as unknown.
Two portraits bordered with gilt above his bed:
his mother and father, stiff in formal dress,
stern, regal, staring beyond revolution
to the Soviet Union they would never see
or see their son escape from. His stare back
falls blunt, yet he sees there is some relation:
aunt, brother, cousins from a distant farm?
Who they were, failed to be, or might have been
fades from the dream-talk of his memory
until the frame itself begins to crack:
so that gazing at them he is like Aeneas
scanning with wonder the images engraved
on Vulcan's shield—they could be children unborn
forecast in pictures, all their destined acts
hanging beyond the mind like a hemorrhage.
Hoisting a bright wool afghan to his shoulder,
lips pressed and flakes of scalp dusting his stoop,
he trembles, scowling, steel-eyed and aroused
for battle, ready to walk through a field
full-blown with bodies and sing out to the tribe.

from *The Threepenny Review*

Song for the In-Itself
and For-Itself

◊   ◊   ◊

The in-itself and for-itself
Were two dimensions of the self.
The in-itself was satisfied
With any crust that fed its pride,
Hinging a self upon the pelf
Which it had smuggled to itself.

The for-itself, its opposite,
Burned with desires infinite;
Nor could it ever find repose,
Allow the boundaries to close
On any possibility.
Preferring anonymity,
It stared into a boundless gulf,
Forever searching for itself.

Like any Ghibelline or Guelph,
The in-itself arranged a self
In some proposed delineation—
A name, identity, or nation,
Accommodating to itself
The views of every other elf.

Meanwhile its counterpart knew all
The aphorisms of Pascal
By heart, and would reflect upon

Our penchant for delusion;
Our infinite capacity
For falsehood and duplicity;
Our vanity, profanity,
Habitual inhumanity;
How all our projects always tend
To come to nothing in the end,
Since what we are is more or less
Projected out of nothingness.
And so on and in similar vein
The for-itself would thus complain,
Abusing mankind for its folly
In litanies of melancholy.
But when the for-itself would rant,
Thinking itself still dominant,
The in-itself would softly creep
Into its bosom, lull it to sleep,
Until at length, its griefs being told,
The inconsolable was consoled
And a new cycle thus began—
Though nothing new beneath the sun.

The in-itself and for-itself
Were two dimensions of the self.
This couplet chorus-like rehearses
The initial premise of these verses.
The self was bitterly divided
And each the other part derided,
With no abatement of their strife
Ensuing while they took in life—
And hence no way of putting closure
Upon our poem's paltry measure.
Enough! We'll leave them on the shelf,
The in-itself and for-itself.

from *Poetry New York*

MICHAEL WHITE

"Camille Monet sur son lit de mort"

◊   ◊   ◊

(for Jackie)

1

Not a picturing. Unclosing landscape
Of disorder: unreadable beneath
The furor of paint, a purely human image
Swims through the scumbled surface of unbeing,
The eyebrows lost in absence. The bluish curve
Of her faint, drawn lips; the bluish glint of her teeth.
Cascading, matted through the loose folds of
Her shroud, the momentary hues of death
Sweep out in nameless energies into
The slippery nuances of reverie:
Blunted silvers, rose and gold dragged clear
Across the flow of canvas. Holding a handful
Of withered violets clutched in an unseen hand.

2

When forty years had passed—in his garden
Slashing stroke by stroke into the dark
Of cataract—he still held one reproach
Against himself. He said: "Nothing is
More natural than the urge to record one last

Image of a person departing this life. . . ."
But nothing could blur the stabbing, recurrent
Memory of his eye as it "searched for
The arrangement of color gradations that death was imposing
On her motionless face. Blue, yellow, gray,
Who knows what else? That was the point I had reached."
It was the last in the series of Camilles—
La femme with the parasol, or in the green
Silk dress; *au bord de l'eau* or *au jardin*—
But this time she has slipped past, into the lighted
Immaterial atmosphere of the bedclothes,
Floating beyond the fine inflections of pain.
This time she slips beyond his streaming skeins
Of paint, her faintly transfixed smile of death
Like a merely spectral scrawl in space, as if,
In the dawn's soft loosening, he tried to wake,
And could not see, and reached for a vanishing dream.

3

Like a coda to the years you clawed death back,
You tried to die four days before you could—
But then found the slim way through. Unsustaining,
Unsustained, your ravished heart sped on
Four days past air and water, breath and blood,
Your face exhausted, drawn, magnificent.
In the moments after, each of us gazed at you
With a nearly unearthly hunger. Frozen blue
In the predawn sky, the lawns of the cul-de-sac
Were framed by the bedside window, and I could see
The stars above, sharp flicks of stars that shimmered
As if in chills of wind. As gently as
I could, I lay beside you, took your hand,
And let your warmth pass slowly into me.

from *The New Republic*

RICHARD WILBUR

A Digression

◇ ◇ ◇

Having confided to the heavy-lipped
Mailbox his great synoptic manuscript,
He stands light-headed in the lingering clang.
How lightly, too, he feels his briefcase hang!

And now it swings beside his knees, as they
From habit start him on his evening way,
With the tranced rhythm of a metronome,
Past hall and grove and stadium toward his home.

Yet as the sun-bathed campus slips behind,
A giddy lack of purpose fills his mind,
Making him swerve into a street which for
Two decades he has managed to ignore.

What stops him in his tracks is that his soul,
Proposing nothing, innocent of goal,
Sees no perspective narrowing between
Gold-numbered doors and frontages of green

But for the moment an obstructive storm
Of specks and flashes that will take no form,
A roiled mosaic or a teeming scrim
That seems to have no pertinence to him.

It is his purpose now as, turning round,
He takes his bearings and is homeward bound,
To ponder what the world's confusion meant
When he regarded it without intent.

from *The New Yorker*

DEAN YOUNG

Upon Hearing of My Friend's Marriage Breaking Up

◊   ◊   ◊

Even in September noon, the groundhog
casts his divining shadow: summer will never
end and when it does it will never come again,
I've only the shadows of doubt, shadows
of a notion. The leaves turn in tarnished
rain like milk. Hearts, rotund with longing
explode like dead horses left in a creek,
our intentions misunderstood, misrepresented
like that day they turned the candles
upside-down, thumped them out and we all
lost our jobs and souls. Nothing personal.
Handshakes around. Of course we're not guilty
of what we've been accused of but
we're guilty of so much else, what's it matter,
I heard on the radio. I hate the radio,
how it pretends to be your friend.
You could be eating, you could be driving around
and then you're screaming, What, what did that fucker say
but by then it's someone else with the voice
of air conditioning saying, Take cover,
storm on the way. It's amazing
word hasn't gotten back to us from irritated
outer space how some creatures of spine and light
have finally had enough. Shut up, they beep back
but we're so dense, so unevolved, we think
it's just the usual interference: Bob next door

blending his Singapore Slings during Wheel
of Fortune. Right now they're working on something
that'll make our fillings fall out,
turn our checking accounts to dust,
something far more definitive.
There's a man starting his mower in the bedroom.
There's a woman burning photos in a sink.
I hate the phone, how it pretends to be
your friend, but I called you anyway,
got some curt, inchoate message that means
everyone's miserable, little shreds of your heart
rain down on me, twitching like slivered worms.
Upstairs, they're overflowing the tub again,
they're doing that Euripidean dance. I knew
a guy in college who stuck his head through a wall.
It seemed to decide something, to make us all
feel grateful, restored to simple things:
cars starting, cottage cheese, Larry, Curly, Moe.
It was, of course, a thin wall, a practice wall,
a wall between nowhere and nowhere's bedroom,
nothing like that 16th century woodcut
where the guy pokes through the sky into
the watchback of the cosmos. Tick, tick.
The cosmos gives me the creeps.
I like a decent chair where you can sit
and order a beer, be smiled at while you wait
for a friend who just had his sutures removed,
who rolls a quarter across his knuckles
to get them working again.

from *The Threepenny Review*

CONTRIBUTORS'
NOTES AND
COMMENTS

DICK ALLEN was born in Troy, New York, in 1939. He is the author of four published volumes, *Flight and Pursuit* (L.S.U., 1987), *Overnight in the Guest House of the Mystic* (L.S.U., 1987), *Regions with No Proper Names* (St. Martin's, 1975), *Anon and Various Time Machine Poems* (Delacorte and Delta, 1971), and has completed two new poetry books, *Touches of Strange* and *The Space Sonnets*—the latter a book-length sonnet sequence he has been writing for twenty-three years. Allen has received grants from the National Endowment for the Arts and the Ingram Merrill Foundation, the Robert Frost Poetry Fellowship, and the Poetry Society of America's Mary Caroline Davis Poetry Prize. He reviews poetry regularly for the *Hudson Review* and the *American Book Review*. In 1990 he guest-edited the "Expansive Poetry" issue of *Crosscurrents*. He is director of creative writing and Charles A. Dana Professor of English at the University of Bridgeport.

Of "A Short History of the Vietnam War Years," Allen writes: "I began this poem intending to mock Surrealistic poetry, with no thought of Vietnam. I thought I'd make as many weird and silly and inconsequential connections as I could in a poem about people in bed. But in the third line, as I relaxed to subconscious associations, the door opening in the mirror brought back Watergate . . . and then when a helicopter flew through it, across the lovers' *flanks* (a military term), the helicopter was the one in which a college classmate was killed in Vietnam. From then on, the poem took me over and I was writing drafts in a semi-trance state for three days. I was back in the sixties and early seventies with the peace movement and the war going on, images of Asia and protest marches intermingling. In those years, it was impossible to separate the war from day-to-day life. Vietnam was in every lovers' bed, its images were pervasive, and our lives seemed continually surreal—ordinary gossip and weather on the TV news and at the end of each evening a New York TV station rolled the names of that day's reported dead in Vietnam across the screen, preceded and followed by commercials for underarm deodorants, toilet bowl cleansers, and dog and cat food. The news from Kent State in May 1970 and within five hours my college campus shut down by students occupying the buildings. . . . Marches on Washington. . . . Vows to never be like our parents. 'And the deltas awoke and flooded Washington.' As the poem ended, the black armband that so many of us wore those years came back, and that strange warfare phrase of *walking mortar fire*, and finally the 'old blind man' whom I probably associate with Lyndon Johnson as he gave his speech announcing he would not run for reelection as president.

"The poem remains unreal and painful to me, its associations and imagery nothing I could have consciously planned—and yet it feels accurate to the sense of those years. The Vietnam War still haunts me; its horrors and effects obsess my life and poetry, the lives of my generation and the generation following mine. We cannot conceive of who we are, of what America and the world is, without thinking of the Vietnam War. The Surrealism I began with an intent of mocking became deadly serious and paradoxically realistic. This is one of those poems in which the poet is used by history, rather than uses it.

"Among many allusions and associations, 'Mai Lai' refers to the My Lai massacre, but is also a woman. 'Tet' is the Tet Offensive that broke the back of American war policy in Vietnam, but is also a man. 'Green meadows' I associate with the green pastures of the Twenty-third Psalm. 'Cambodia' alludes to the incursion into Vietnam's neighboring country, and 'People's Park' was the California site of many peace protests. The wind from Ohio brings back the killings at Kent State University.

"As I worked over the poem years after I began it, it emerged as basically iambic and trochaic pentameter, with a few lines longer or shorter. (Some of the technique seems ironically reminiscent of Stephen Spender's 'I Think Continually of Those Who Were Truly Great,' a poem on which I wrote a forty-page paper when I was a Syracuse University undergraduate.) What I wanted was a predominance of stresses, to make it impossible to read the poem quickly. I wanted it to have a backward pull, the iambics and some anapests wanting to break free, to relax, but never able to, held by the mortar fire of trochaics and spondees—as the lovers—as we—could not break free for all those years. And still cannot."

TOM ANDREWS was born in Charleston, West Virginia, in 1961. He is the author of *The Brother's Country*, a winner in the National Poetry Series (Persea Books, 1990), and *The Hemophiliac's Motorcycle*, which won the 1993 Iowa Poetry Prize (University of Iowa Press, 1994), He edited *On William Stafford: The Worth of Local Things*, a collection of essays and book reviews (University of Michigan Press, 1993). In 1993 he received a fellowship from the National Endowment for the Arts. Currently he teaches at Ohio University and lives in Lancaster, Ohio.

Of "Cinema Vérité," Andrews writes: "My first two books are rather serious and elegiac; they deal often with my brother's experience with kidney disease and his eventual death, and with my own experience with hemophilia. After I finished my second book, I knew that, while I wanted to resist 'turning against' the earlier work, I also wanted to write out of a different impulse. I've always loved and admired writers—like Rabelais, Sterne, Queneau, O'Brien, among others—who celebrate a fearless, undogmatic, comic sense of life. 'Cinema Vérité' represents my attempt to write out of that love and admiration.

" 'Cinema Vérité' is the overarching title of a book of similar prose pieces, all in the form of film scripts. The three reprinted here are among the first I wrote. I owe a substantial debt to Stuart Friebert, co-editor of *Field*, who suggested that I try writing prose poems. Without his gentle nudge, which happened to arrive as I was reading the 'unfilmable scenarios' of Benjamin Fondane and other Surrealists, I might never have pursued the film script form, with which I have had so much fun."

JOHN ASHBERY was born in Rochester, New York, in 1927. He is the author of fifteen books of poetry, including *And the Stars Were Shining* (Farrar, Straus & Giroux, 1994) and *Flow Chart* (Knopf, 1991). *Self-Portrait in a Convex Mirror* (Viking, 1975) received the Pulitzer Prize for poetry as well as the National Book Critics Circle Award and the National Book Award. A collection of his art criticism, *Reported Sightings*, was published by Knopf in 1989. He has delivered the Charles Eliot Norton lectures at Harvard University and is currently the Charles P. Stevenson, Jr., Professor of Languages and Literature at Bard College. He was the guest editor of *The Best American Poetry 1988*.

BURLIN BARR was born in Waxahachie, Texas, in 1963. He lives in upstate New York and is poetry editor of *Epoch*.

Barr writes: "I'm fond of a particular recording of 'A Night in Tunisia' that is saturated with live sounds. At moments, Charlie Parker's phrasing is almost lost to the background. And, throughout, a dog is barking.

"I don't claim—nor do I attempt—to transcribe or describe such things. However, I think these kinds of moments offer their own clarity. Though most statements and actions contain guides or kernels—vaguely articulated imperatives or even unlisted ones—learning about these guides is always elusive. Of course, excessive elements do not refer to such imperatives, but perhaps they can indicate them. They may broaden the field. After our wished-for clear perceptions have combined with all the attendant unrelated and hard-to-place things, the original object of our attention inevitably changes and perhaps even falters.

"Although 'Tremendous Mood Swings' does not articulate any of this, it participates in it. It does not describe this kind of excess but, typically, suffers under and thrives on it."

CYNTHIA BOND was born in Stoneham, Massachusetts, in 1961. She was raised and educated in Illinois. A recent graduate of Cornell Law School, she is currently practicing law in Ithaca, New York.

Bond writes: " 'What You Want Means What You Can Afford' is one of a series of lyric poems, the product of a period during which I wrote a poem every day before leaving the office where I worked. I began to view the day as a collection of refuse that I would pick through to make a poem. The poem became a receptacle for the day's events, visions, thoughts, and found language. Nearly all the poems in the series function by way of poetic conceit. I especially like this poem because the conceit is so thick that its subject is almost completely obscured; meaning is little of the matter."

CATHERINE BOWMAN was born in El Paso, Texas, in 1957. She grew up in San Antonio, where she worked as a journalist. She attended the graduate writing program at Columbia University. Her collec-

tion of poems *1-800-HOT-RIBS* (Gibbs Smith, 1993) won the Pere-
grine Smith Poetry Prize. Her work was included in the 1989 edition
of *The Best American Poetry*. She lives and teaches in New York
City.

Of "Demographics," Bowman writes: "I thought of the title for
this poem when I had a job editing research proposals for a consor-
tium of *Fortune* 500 social scientists who had designed a five-step
program to solve all of society's problems. During regular spell-
checks, the word 'demographics' would frequently show up as
'demongraphics.'

"I saw the poem as one continuous block, not to be broken up
into stanzas. It is a kind of flip-book. It is meant to be read very
fast."

GEORGE BRADLEY was born in Roslyn, New York, in 1953. His first
book of verse, *Terms to Be Met*, was published by Yale University
Press in 1986. His second, *Of the Knowledge of Good and Evil*, came
out from Knopf in 1991. He hopes someday to have a third, to
which the poem appearing in this anthology would contribute the
title.

Bradley writes: "Regarding 'The Fire Fetched Down,' I had
wished for quite a while to write something in exploration of the
sad fact that *Homo sapiens*, the thinking animal, wants nothing so
much as not to have to think; but I had lacked the right vehicle for
such philosophical freight. The occasion to attempt the poem came
when I stumbled across the etymology of the name 'Prometheus.'
The reworking of Greek myth is an unsurprising stratagem, of
course, but it remains one of our best. From Virgil down to Freud,
it seems that the most ambitious imaginative work in Western
culture has in many ways been a mere amplification of those tall
tales first told by firelight some three thousand years ago."

CHARLES BUKOWSKI (1920–1994) was born in Andernach, Germany.
He was brought to the United States at the age of three, was
raised in Los Angeles, and lived in San Pedro, California. He told a
magazine interviewer that he began drinking at age thirteen because
of the continual beatings he suffered at the hands of his father. He
moved to New York City in 1941. Trying to make it as a writer, he
supported himself variously as a dishwasher, truck driver, mailman,
parking lot attendant, elevator operator, and Red Cross orderly. In

1946 he embarked on a period devoted to drinking and travel. Ten years later he resumed writing and enjoyed his first measure of success. He is the author of forty-five books of poetry and prose, including *Notes of a Dirty Old Man*, *Post Office*, *Women*, and *Ham on Rye*. He wrote the screenplay for Barbet Schroeder's movie *Barfly*, a portrait of the poet—played by Mickey Rourke—as a young man. Bukowski's latest published books are *The Last Night of the Earth Poems* (Black Sparrow Press, 1993) and *Screams from the Balcony: Selected Letters 1960–1970*, ed. Seamus Cooney (Black Sparrow, 1993). He died of leukemia on March 9, 1994. He had just completed the manuscript of *Pulp*, a detective novel.

In a letter to Carl Weissner dated "November what 18?, 1966" (published in *Screams from the Balcony*), Bukowski wrote: "it is only when the artist is dead that the masses enjoy his suffering and go to warm movies and eat popcorn and enjoy it. I was guilty of it myself. I remember when I was in the Village I went to see a movie about the life of Verdi. if I remember, there was a part there where he got a bag of nuts from an old woman in the street. he was starving. I like that. I have starved many times trying to cut some insignia into the cement. I shouldn't have liked it, the Verdi thing. but then when he came back famous with the beautiful woman at his side and he gave the old woman a batch of money for the bag of nuts that night, I didn't care for that too much. he was defaming her act, showing off to his broad. he should have taken the old woman to his place and fucked her and drank wine with her and asked her to talk to him across the kitchen table. but then Verdi was not perfect. I make some mistakes myself."

REBECCA BYRKIT was born in Phoenix in 1960. Her poems have appeared in *New England Review*, *Ploughshares*, and *Pacific Coast Review*, and she has completed a poetry manuscript entitled *zealand*, which will be published by Sun/Gemini Press in 1995. In 1992 she received her M.F.A. at the University of Arizona, where she teaches film rhetoric and creative writing. She was awarded a 1993–1994 poetry fellowship from the Arizona Commission on the Arts. She is the director of the New Tucson Writers' Conference.

Of "The Only Dance There Is," Byrkit writes: "After a long bleak spell this poem exploded from me as a veritable orgy of opportunity. 'Dance' is a dervish tribute to the phenomenon of being helplessly drawn to catastrophic relationships and an aesthetic developed of crisis, sex, wine-from-a-box, and language. In my moment of criminal need to compose this poem I called upon various narrative elements I'd tried to include in my previous poems: the setting of the Mountainaire Tavern near Flagstaff where I'd 'lived' for many years, and a satisfyingly crass reference to the suicide of a, um, I don't know if 'boyfriend' is the word—which had happened about a year before. The resulting voice felt like a streak—ballistic and finite and, as it turned out, vastly liberating."

AMY CLAMPITT was born in New Providence, Iowa, in 1920. She graduated from Grinnell College and has since lived mainly in New York City, with stints of teaching at William and Mary, Amherst, and Smith. Her books of poetry include *The Kingfisher* (1983), *What the Light Was Like* (1985), *Archaic Figure* (1987), *Westward* (1990), and *A Silence Opens* (1994), all published by Knopf. *Predecessors, Et Cetera* appeared in the University of Michigan Press's Poets on Poetry Series in 1991. A play, *Mad with Joy*, concerning the life and times of Dorothy Wordsworth, was given a staged reading by the Poets' Theater in Cambridge, Massachusetts, in March 1993.

Of "A Catalpa Tree on West Twelfth Street," Clampitt writes: "The summer solstice has been a recurring subject for me. When *The New York Times* let it be known that its op-ed page would give space to poetry on midsummer day, a poem I'd written several years earlier came to mind. I dug it out and was given pause by a little clump of references—e.g., to punk rock and TV dinners—that had to do all too unmistakably with some other, bygone solstice, and were thus hardly fit for mention in a daily paper. After due reflection, the passage was rewritten to encompass 'grunge, hip-hop, Chinese takeout, co-ops.' That last, of course, can't be called the latest thing as of June 21, 1993, and will in any event have had no particularly vivid relevance for anyone who has not personally withstood the vagaries of real estate in New York City. So far as the catalpa tree itself is concerned, such minute contemporaneity is an anachronism: it has by now reached the evident limits of its growth, and its coming demise has become the subject of another poem."

MICHELLE T. CLINTON was born in Bridgeport, Connecticut, in 1954. She was raised in Los Angeles, where she lives, though she plans to relocate to northern California. She has had no academic literary training. In 1992 she received a fellowship from the National Endowment for the Arts. Her two books are *Good Sense and the Faithless* (1994) and *High Blood/Pressure* (1987), both from West End Press.

Of "Tantrum Girl Responds to Death," Clinton writes: "The form is my greatest source of joy in this particular work. The form, which I borrowed from a text by a Chicana poet published in *ZYZZYVA*, answered the question 'How can this poem tell a story without the linear, ideological, and consequently manipulative aspects of traditional fiction?'

"The content of the piece is rooted in a moment when political, metaphysical, and personal forces condensed inside the movement of my life. I lost control. I felt like a crazy poet, uplifted and plagued by an insight that would cause me to scream, an insight that would validate and then isolate me: my outrage at the hypocrisy, the silence and lies of our society. This rage is typical of my work. I was happy that I could use the language of the gay world, happy that I could contain that language in an African-American cultural context, and pleased that I use one word from Jewish culture. (I'm into the crosscultural, polyethnic thing. I believe it is our important hope, our only direction.)

"Still, I cannot say that I understand the persona of the piece. She is strange to me. I anticipate the future lessons of my work, the other forms, the stories and poems, that will teach me about the energy that carries me, my will intact, through my life."

JAMES CUMMINS was born in Columbus, Ohio, in 1948, and grew up in Cleveland and Indianapolis. He is curator of the Elliston Poetry Collection at the University of Cincinnati, where he teaches literature and writing. *The Whole Truth*, his book of sestinas about Perry Mason and his crew, was published by North Point Press in 1986. He has received grants from the National Endowment for the Arts, the Ingram Merrill Foundation, and the Ohio Arts Council. He conceives of identity as fluid, and was once a baseball player and a spy—no, wait, that was Moe Berg.

Of "Sestina," Cummins writes: "This poem came out of the confluence of a leave, a depression, and winter. I willed myself to go back to things I had barred and padlocked away—then wheel them out in another kind of cage, the sestina. I think the sestina is a marvelous way to contain and form prose rhythms, absurdity, narrative, argument. It may sound silly, but the sestina taught me how to think in poetry. It taught me *what comes next*—instead of having to wait for months, or years, while I figured it out for myself."

RAMOLA DHARMARAJ was born in Madras, India, in 1964. She studied physics and business at the University of Madras and worked as a freelance journalist in India. She received an M.F.A. in poetry from George Mason University, where she edited *Phoebe* for a year. She has taught literature and composition at George Mason University, George Washington University, and Montgomery College, and currently makes a living as a technical writer at the American Red Cross. She has completed a first manuscript of poetry, *Invisible Season*, and is working now on both poetry and fiction.

Of "full of rain, the word," Dharmaraj writes: "Sometimes poems coalesce in ways you least expect them to. I had been thinking about concepts of god, both the Hindu pantheon and the Judeo-Christian versions of god, and the poetic notion of the word as god in a very literal sense, which led me to think about language itself, its empowerments and exclusions. I was also thinking about the great disparities between the urban and the rural worlds. The language of experience in most of the world, which is poor and rural, lives at such a great socioeconomic and psychological distance from urban, especially Western, reality that it has become acceptable in the West to decry that experience and relegate the disparate whole of it to the arbitrary and conveniently alien status of another dimension, the 'Third World.' I wrote out of resistance—I began to envisage the word as rising out of human reality, out of suffering and work and survival, as opposed to descending from the heavens in a show of divine benevolence; god as powerless, and the Christian concept of the word emerging not from the colonizing imperatives of evangelism but as if inevitably from the lives of the very poor and powerless among the peoples of the colonized world, not seeking to impose power but imprinting nevertheless on urban consciousness. The question of course as to the depth and nature of this imprint on the small fraction of urban elites who can afford a distant Second Coming is an old one yet is what the poem led me to—centuries of hierarchy impose silences that we who partake of the privileges of the world too easily become accustomed to. The image that began the poem and carried it for me was that of the monsoon, which agricultural India relies on as the only major source of rain every year."

THOMAS M. DISCH was born in Des Moines, Iowa, in 1940 and was bred in various parts of Minnesota. *The Priest: A Gothic Romance* (Knopf, 1995) continues a sequence of novels that began with *The Businessman: A Tale of Terror* (Berkley) and continued with *The M.D.: A Horror Story* (Berkley). A fourth novel, *The Sub: A Study in Witchcraft*, is in the works. His most recent collection of poems is *Dark Verses and Light* (Johns Hopkins, 1991). A former vice president of the National Book Critics Circle, he is a drama critic for the *New York Daily News*.

Of "The Cardinal Detoxes," Disch writes: "In spring 1987 I began to review theater for *The Nation*, and not long after that, emboldened by both a sense of the sheer, room-for-one-more size of the entertainment industry and by what seemed to me a heartening shortage of good writing, I tried my hand as a playwright. First, at the invitation of Jeffrey Cohen, who headed the RAPP Theater on Manhattan's Lower East Side, I wrote an adaptation, in four acts (though with only one intermission), of General Lew Wallace's *Ben-Hur*. In my version Wallace acts as a Wilderesque Stage Manager and doubles in some of the roles, so that the original melodrama, while remaining intact, is interleaved with material relating to Wallace's Civil War career and to later Roman/American imperial parallels. RAPP premiered *Ben-Hur* in Baltimore in the early summer of 1989, and not long afterward, dazzled by having seen *Ben-Hur* with its sets and costumes and original musical score and a cast of over twenty, I began to write a play that would be all my own—not an adaptation—*The Vampires, A Comedy in Two Acts*—and halfway through *that* play, around Labor Day, I was interrupted by another brainstorm, and in a ten-day marathon, sequestered in a cottage in the Poconos, I wrote *The Cardinal Detoxes*.

"I doubt it would have been written without the confidence imparted by *Ben-Hur* and the momentum achieved in *The Vampires*, for in terms of practical producibility *The Cardinal Detoxes* would seem a pretty quixotic venture—a thirty-five-minute monologue in blank verse designed to serve as a vehicle for my hoard of opinions concerning the secret, *Realpolitik* reasons for the Catholic Church's more opprobrious policies and scandalous behavior. Like so many other fervent ex-Catholics, the Church's misdeeds were my hobby-horse, but I'd never *ridden* that hobbyhorse for any distance. However, I did already have the 'voice' of the play's protagonist, who'd first appeared as a Machiavellian Cardinal in four short poetic monologues. When the idea came to me for the play's dramatic premise, which gives the Cardinal a compelling reason to take inventory of the Church's entire can of worms, the work went wonderfully smoothly. No doubt I was helped by my conviction that this would be a closet drama, unlikely to be published, certain never to be performed.

"With an impresario's instinct for scandal, Jeffrey Cohen decided to pair *The Cardinal Detoxes* with an even shorter Grand Guignol curtain-raiser I'd written some time before, *The Audition*, and to perform that on RAPP's smaller stage. Cohen had the perfect Cardinal ready to hand in the person of George McGrath, a RAPP veteran, who had taken the role of Lew Wallace in *Ben-Hur*. Some nine months after it was written, on May 23, 1990, the show opened at RAPP's home in a former parochial school building on East 4th Street.

"Ultimately it was to be the play's venue, more than its contents, that would make it the focus of controversy. In its initial three-week run, the Church hurled no thunderbolts at *The Cardinal Detoxes*, placing its trust, prudently, in the normal mortality rate of Off-Off-Broadway productions. The play got a good amount of critical attention but not the make-or-break authentication of notice by *The New York Times*. *Theater Week*, however, concluded a rave review with the suggestion that the play might serve as 'an ideal midnight show that just might be *The Rocky Horror Picture Show* of Off-Off-Broadway,' and in September Jeffrey Cohen decided to revive the play (without *The Audition*) as per *Theater Week*'s suggestion, for an open-ended run. Before performances could resume RAPP received a letter from the lawyers of its landlord, the Most Holy Redeemer Church, demanding that RAPP terminate all performances of the play, because it contained 'language . . . which would be detrimental to Landlord's reputation as a Roman Catholic Church.' If the play went on, RAPP would be evicted, along with the more than thirty theater groups, artists, and social service organizations that sublet space in the former school building from RAPP.

"On September 20, 1990, the Church's threat made headlines

in *The New York Times*, the *Post*, and *Newsday*, with Cardinal O'Connor's press agent, Joseph Zwilling, putting the Church's case. 'This is detrimental to the Catholic Church. Even though it is rented by an outside group, we still have to run it in keeping with Church teachings. We include a clause in the lease to insure that.'

"When RAPP went to court to fight the eviction, media attention warmed up. The *Post*, where O'Connor's least sneeze is accorded front-page attention, ran an editorial on September 23, entitled 'The Church Fights Back,' congratulating the archdiocese on 'its principled stand' and concluding that 'the priests and lay members of the Church should know that New Yorkers of all faiths admire the manner in which they've conducted themselves.'

"In the next month I used up most of my allotted fifteen minutes of fame, as my first-ever soundbite was aired on WINS All-News radio, and on Channels 5 and 2, and in the *Post*. 'The Church has always been in the habit of trying to smash unflattering mirrors. If you write anything about the Church that's not a vehicle for Bing Crosby they go ape.' I also had the pleasure of publishing an open letter to Cardinal O'Connor in the October 15 issue of *The Nation*. With more time than is allowed in a soundbite, I posed the rhetorical question: 'When criticism is based upon matters of public record, scandal and notoriety (and all the fictive scandals referred to in my play have clear parallels in news reports of the past few years), can the *critic* be blamed for damaging the Church's reputation?' I went on, 'The themes *The Cardinal Detoxes* does treat—the *Realpolitik* behind the Church's positions on abortion, AIDS education, shrinking parishes, diminishing vocations, women's aspirations for the priesthood, and the hierarchy's ingrained hypocrisy—are the regular concern of most articulate, liberal Catholics (they do exist, though increasingly they are leaving the Church—or being evicted). Witness almost any issue of *National Catholic Reporter*, the nation's foremost independent Catholic journal. Yet what is common knowledge in the pages of the *Reporter* has been decreed forbidden fruit on the stage of RAPP.'

"The story hit the papers again on October 5, when Irma Santaella of the State Supreme Court ruled in the Church's favor, at which point enough media energy had been generated that the celebrity attorney William Kunstler took up RAPP's cause, and he, Jeffrey Cohen, and I were taken to New Jersey to appear on a daytime talk show hosted by Curtis Sliwa, of Guardian Angel fame, who, in lieu of an official spokesman, undertook to argue the Church's case—and did so rather more ably than Zwilling.

"Later in October there was a final spate of headlines when the Church, balked of the gratification of an immediate closing of the play because of the appeals process, apparently summoned a goon squad from the City's Department of Buildings, who tried to close the theater by force, provoking a near-riot. As reported in the *Times*, a Department of Buildings spokesman said its action was coincidental and caused by clerical [sic] error: 'There absolutely was no intervention by the archdiocese.' Kunstler expressed a contrary opinion, to which Zwilling retorted with his reflexive response to any criticism: 'Ridiculous.'

"In the end the Church carried the day by its traditional means— inertia and patience. The controversy lost steam, the case dragged on in court, audiences dwindled, and the *coup de grâce* came not at the hands of the Church but by the provisions of Actors Equity, which requires any production that runs beyond a certain length of time to up salaries and hire more personnel. RAPP vacated the premises and ceased to exist. Jeffrey Cohen moved to the West Coast, where he recently directed a well-received *As You Like It*. I am now writing a novel, *The Priest: A Gothic Romance*, which has served as a more than sufficient safety valve for any residue of anger from the experience. Indeed, I must admit that, having been spared direct physical confrontation (unlike Cohen, who told me he had been roughed up by 'workmen' trying to close down the theater), I found the whole thing pretty exhilarating.

"When things had calmed down I often wondered *why* such a fuss was made about a half-hour-long verse drama playing at the far reaches of Off-Off-Broadway. Why did the Church *bother*? I have two theories. The paranoid theory is that the Church hoped to set a precedent with this case that would allow it to exert its power as a landlord in sinister new ways. If RAPP could have its First Amendment rights abrogated by a clause in a rental lease, might not other clauses be inserted in other leases to (for instance) bar pharmacies from selling contraceptives—or even to allow the Church as a residential landlord to evict any tenant who has had an abortion?

"Actually I don't really think the tide is running that way. I think that what happened with *The Cardinal Detoxes* was simply a testimony to the primal power of live theater, which can generate public controversy out of all proportion to the size of its audiences. When the Church acted to shut down my play, I doubt that it had been seen at that point by as many as a thousand people. But the Church, with dinosaur-like intuition, understands that the transaction between players and audience is essentially the same as that between priest and worshippers. Basically we're in competition for the same souls, as our Puritan forefathers realized when they targeted the theaters of their time. In the crucial political act of forming and controlling the moral imagination they would brook no rivals. The Puritans lost that round. I think the Church is losing this one."

MARK DOTY was born in Tennessee in 1953. He has published three books of poems, *Turtle, Swan* (Godine, 1987), *Bethlehem in Broad Daylight* (Godine, 1991), and *My Alexandria* (University of Illinois Press, 1993), which was chosen by Philip Levine for the National Poetry Series. *My Alexandria* won both the *Los Angeles Times* Book Prize and the National Book Critics Circle Award in poetry for 1993. He has received fellowships from the Ingram Merrill Foundation and the National Endowment for the Arts. He teaches at Sarah Lawrence College and in the M.F.A. Program at Vermont College, and lives in Provincetown, Massachusetts.

Of "Difference," Doty writes: "After wrestling all morning with a poem that just wouldn't come right, I went for a walk along the shore, where I encountered a whole flotilla of jellyfish, a lesson in mutability and grace. When I got home I found that they'd replaced whatever poem it was I had been trying to shape, and over the course of a day or two 'Difference' seemed to write itself. It's a poem that tries to think about the slippery, shape-shifting nature of words themselves, which can only be metaphors for what they represent. Language itself is as slippery, undulant, and unreliable as the uncapturable world it attempts to fix. I hope my poem suggests that this unreliability might be cause for celebration—and perhaps reason to work all the harder at the project of making meaning in language, instead of giving up on the idea altogether."

DENISE DUHAMEL was born in Woonsocket, Rhode Island, in 1961. She received a New York Foundation for the Arts Fellowship in 1989 and a Poets & Writers "Writers Exchange" award, representing Pennsylvania, in 1993. Her work has appeared in *The Best*

American Poetry 1993 and in *Mondo Barbie*. She is the author of *Smile!* (Warm Spring Press, Harrisburg, Pennsylvania, 1993) and *The Woman with Two Vaginas*, a series of poems based on Inuit folklore (Salmon Run Press, Anchorage, Alaska, 1994.) She lives in Lewisburg, Pennsylvania, with her husband, the poet Nick Carbo.

Duhamel writes: "I wanted to write about bulimia—the horrors specific to it as opposed to other, also horrible, eating disorders. I gathered stories of binges and purges from several women and one man. These stories and my own struggles with the disease all interwove into the one character who wanted to speak—and also, I suppose, not speak—in 'Bulimia.' A bulimic episode is probably one of the most private and shameful of human experiences, and perhaps that is why many bulimics can block such experiences from their conscious waking lives, sometimes for years at a time. Yet what I wanted to capture is the bulimic who is aware of her bulimia in scientific and psychological ways, the bulimic who has read up on her madness and still can't stop. That is why the poem is written in the third person rather than the first person—the bulimic is looking at herself as an outsider."

TONY ESOLEN was born in Scranton, Pennsylvania, in 1959. He was educated at Princeton (B.A., 1981) and the University of North Carolina (Ph.D., 1987). He teaches Renaissance literature at Providence College in Rhode Island. *Peppers*, a volume of poetry, came out in 1991 (New Poets Series). Johns Hopkins University Press will publish his translation of *De Rerum Natura* of Lucretius.

Esolen writes: "I grew up in northeastern Pennsylvania, in a small town whose main industry used to be coal mining but now is booze. The surrounding hills are broken up with big old stripping holes and heaps of coal dust called 'culm.' You dump dead cars into one and ride dirt bikes up the other. If you grow up in such a town, you don't go to college, or if you do, you stick around and get a job as a welder anyway. Everyone in the town is Italian, Polish, Russian, or Irish. Everyone eats spaghetti and pierogi and drinks beer. Everyone eventually becomes a Little League coach. As everywhere, people are born, they fall in love, they die, and then they're forgotten.

"If I had it to do over again, I wouldn't have grown up in any other place. Not that I'm a typical machine-oil-and-guts working-class poet. I studied literature at Princeton and Chapel Hill, finally majoring in the Renaissance, with a strong emphasis backwards into the Middle Ages and the Latin classics. Nowadays I pound out an article or two a year on Renaissance history and Spenser, for which I've been rewarded with that ticket to academic heaven, tenure. And studying Renaissance literature has taught me about form and balance, about rhetorical twists, about setting up 'laws' by way of metrical or generic expectations in order to violate them, about the human need to tell stories and create universal myths. That training has been necessary for me. But when I incorporate what the Renaissance teaches me back into the twentieth century, I try (and Lord knows how often I fail) to resist the dead hand of academia and write about the life I know, *for* the people who have to live that life. It means shifting my audience from lovers of Milton to that vast majority of people—often exceedingly intelligent—for whom poetry is as distant a thing as Pluto. This is the audience I have in mind for poems such as 'Northwestern Mathematics'—not Milton's 'fit readers though few' but persons of wit and taste who may not be schooled in the traditions of verse, but who understand how beautiful it is to go fishing in a place where almost nothing besides human folly can survive.

"So here's where I stand, a classicist who hates aesthetic elitism, struggling to reintroduce Renaissance mythmaking not for the literati but for anybody who likes to read. Maybe a vain endeavor, maybe not. Who knows. In the meantime, I'm perfectly happy living with my wife, Debra (who is also my agent and best critic), our baby daughter, Jessica, and our dog, Oliver, who amazes his friends and confounds his enemies. He knows, too, that he's more important than any poem."

RICHARD FOERSTER was born in the Bronx, New York, in 1949, and earned degrees from Fordham College and the University of Virginia. He was awarded the "Discovery"/*The Nation* Prize in 1985 and *Poetry's* Bess Hokin Prize in 1992. His two collections of poetry are *Sudden Harbor* (1992) and *Patterns of Descent* (1993), both published by Orchises Press. He lives in York Beach, Maine, where he works as a freelance educational writer and editor and as a typesetter. Since 1978 he has been an associate editor of *Chelsea*.

Of "Life Drawing," Foerster writes: "Like so many of my poems, this one is about transformation, but also about the paradox of communion, the miracle that occurs when apparent opposites are fused in a ritualized instant—each aspiring to become the other, each drawing life from the other. So there they stand: the naked young man and the observer—each transformed against the backdrop of that 'immaculate void' where art and religion begin. To say more would strip them both of mystery and would dress up the poem with more clothing than it deserves."

ALICE FULTON was born in Troy, New York, in 1952. She is currently a fellow of the John D. and Catherine T. MacArthur Foundation. Her fourth book will be published by Norton in 1995. Her previous volumes are *Powers of Congress* (David R. Godine, 1990), *Palladium* (University of Illinois, 1986), and *Dance Script with Electric Ballerina* (University of Pennsylvania Press, 1983). She is a professor of English at the University of Michigan, Ann Arbor.

Fulton writes: "My husband, Hank De Leo, is a painter. His remarks about the technical aspects of working with oils suggested the metaphorical surround of several poems. From talking with him, I learned that the painter prepares the canvas for oils by creating a barrier of gesso that stands between the linen and the pigment. This process—of creating a protective gesso scrim—spoke to (or led to) several of my recent fascinations. 'The Priming Is a Negligee' thinks about interruptions, boundary, immersion, and façade. The surface is the subject in more than one sense.

"Of course, as long as there are boundaries, there will be otherness. And as long as there is otherness, there will be war and alienation. Yet boundaries also are necessary (of course!) to perception, biology, and constructions of the self. Some of my new work considers the power of recombinant boundaries—the crossover of DNA; metamorphoses; or androgyny, for instance. I've taken to calling the erasure or blurring of borders 'immersion.' In a broad aesthetic sense, I'm interested in what gives: in stretch or elasticity. This poem is a bit different in that it sees walls (i.e., the boundaries of gesso, sunscreen, leading, sheets) as shields against an abnegating immersion. It's the protective gesso between the canvas and the painting that allows the image to endure.

"Many of my poems try to dismantle or interrogate dichotomies—including the foreground-background, subject-object, spirit-matter, mind-body, culture-nature, and male-female alignments. Rather than reinforce dualistic categories, I try to suggest thirdness (or multiplicity) as what comes between binary modes of thought.

In 'The Priming Is a Negligee,' the 'between' quality (of gesso, sunshade, fabric) disrupts the binary (of canvas/image, body/sun, self/other). I like the force of 'between' for its interruptive as well as its archival qualities.

"Emily Dickinson's comment 'I find I need more veil' has intrigued me for some years. Her words reverberated in my mind as I wrote. I also wanted to question the concept of light as the great positive. In this poem, light is a corrosive force. And at last and at first, I was entranced by the possibilities of language—always, always: a veil in itself."

ALLISON FUNK was born in Princeton, New Jersey, in 1951. She received an M.F.A. from Columbia University and now teaches writing and literature at Southern Illinois University at Edwardsville. She has received a fellowship from the National Endowment for the Arts and the George Kent Prize from *Poetry*. Her book of poems, *Forms of Conversion*, was published by Alice James Books in 1986. She has recently completed a new manuscript entitled *Living at the Epicenter*.

Funk writes: "In 1990, I moved from the coast of Massachusetts to Edwardsville, a little town on the Illinois side of the Mississippi River. From the beginning, I was determined to put aside my love for the ocean, to discover the Mississippi and make it part of me. Somehow it seemed vital to exchange one body of water for another. Newly divorced, I was determined not to fall in love again. These desires met in the making of 'After Dark.'

"The poem was written over a two-year period (1991 and 1992), before the great flood that devastated the river towns in the Midwest during the summer of 1993. In its disastrous flooding, the Mississippi showed me another aspect of itself, one at odds with my metaphor of the patient lover."

JORIE GRAHAM was born in New York City in 1950. She grew up in Italy, studied in French schools, and attended the Sorbonne, New York University, Columbia University, and the University of Iowa. She has published five books of poetry: *Hybrids of Plants and of Ghosts* (1980) and *Erosion* (1983), from Princeton University Press, and *The End of Beauty* (1987), *Region of Unlikeness* (1991), and *Materialism* (1993), from the Ecco Press. She has received a MacArthur Fellowship and the Morton Dauwen Zabel Award from the American Academy of Arts and Letters. She lives in Iowa City with her husband and daughter, and teaches at the University of Iowa's Writers' Workshop. She was the guest editor of *The Best American Poetry 1990*.

DEBORA GREGER was born in Walsenburg, Colorado, in 1949. She is the author of three books of poetry published by Princeton University Press: *Movable Islands* (1980), *And* (1986), and *The 1002nd Night* (1990). A new collection, *Off-Season at the Edge of the World*, appeared in 1994 from the University of Illinois Press. She has lived in Cambridge, England. She teaches in the creative writing program at the University of Florida at Gainesville.

DONALD HALL was born in New Haven, Connecticut, in 1928. He lives with his wife, the poet Jane Kenyon, in New Hampshire, and makes his living as a freelance writer. His eleven books of poetry include *The Museum of Clear Ideas* (Ticknor & Fields, 1993) and a book-length poem, *The One Day* (Ticknor & Fields, 1988), which won the National Book Critics Circle Prize in poetry. *Their Ancient Glittering Eyes* (Ticknor & Fields, 1992) expanded and revised his *Remembering Poets* (1978). *Life Work*, an essay, was recently published by Beacon Press. He was the guest editor of *The Best American Poetry 1989*.

Of "Another Elegy," Hall writes: "James Wright died in 1980. A year later, I started an elegy that I worked on for seven years. It was ambitious; I called it 'Another Elegy' because it was traditional—and because, being a rueful sort, I had written many elegies. I made draft after draft, and every now and then thought that I finished it. There was a skinny-lined version, about 1984, that I almost published. But I kept realizing, anew, that the poem failed. I went off on tangents, and some tangents ended in *The One Day* and 'Praise for Death.' In 1988 I finished another version and showed it to a friend who wrote me a letter that fixed or completed my own disgust. I decided never to look at the poem again. I put it away, after more than five hundred drafts.

"For two years I managed not to think about 'Another Elegy' Then for a year it kept squirming back into my head; I told it to go away; it kept twitching—and I arrived at a new strategy for the poem.

"Many more friends had died; I lost some colon to cancer. I

decided to make 'Another Elegy' not for James Wright but for a generic *poète maudit* of our generation. I found the old manuscript and set to work again. The first day I made enormous changes, writing into it, at it, and around it for three or four hours. Ray Carver, John Logan, and Dick Hugo entered 'William Trout,' joining James Wright. As I continued, the living also infiltrated the poem: Robert Bly, Galway Kinnell, Louis Simpson. . . . Finally I noted the figure lamented at the center of the elegy—the figure (it has been observed) lamented at the center of every elegy—who is the elegist himself.

"In three or four months, I finished the poem printed here. Normally I take a fair amount of time to write a poem, and many drafts, but this is the poem that has taken the most drafts of all. (A draft is merely a retyping; sometimes the changes are small.) Hard labor does not make a poem *good*—but it makes it memorable to the poet. Also, it is possible that method of long attention—writing over years, revisiting the poem thousands of mornings—alters the manner of making. One morning I looked for an image of the old autumn's leaves as they emerge from snow at the end of winter; the usual dead metaphors derive from fabric: *tattered, lacy*. The word 'fishbone' came to mind, without a notion of its possible utility except as a visual image. I tried it out; a week later I noticed—all through my poem about a man named Trout—the fishermen and hooks; a tracheotomy like a gill; sharks, pickerel, and catfish, which is to say bullhead and horned pout."

FORREST HAMER was born in Goldsboro, North Carolina, in 1956. He lives in Oakland, California, where he works as a psychologist. He was educated at Yale (B.A.) and at Berkeley (Ph.D.). Poems from a manuscript in progress have appeared in *ZYZZYVA*, *Muleteeth*, and *Berkeley Poetry Review*. "Getting Happy" was his first appearance in print.

Of "Getting Happy," Hamer writes: "As I began to write myself past a years-long 'block,' I became once again interested in the reasons we sometimes fear surrender to what or who moves us. Some of the reasons became clearer as I reflected on some of my childhood experiences in the black, southern church, a place where people of all ages gathered through spirit to surrender to each other."

LYN HEJINIAN was born in 1941 in northern California. She is the co-editor (with Barrett Watten) of *Poetics Journal*, and the author of many books, most recently *Oxota: A Short Russian Novel* (The Figures, 1991) and *The Cell* (Sun & Moon Press, 1992). A new collection will be published by Sun & Moon in 1994 under the title *The Cold of Poetry*. Two volumes of her translations from the work of the Russian poet Arkadii Dragomoshchenko have been published by Sun & Moon Press, *Description* (1990) and *Xenia* (1994). She is a member of the Poetics Faculty at New College of California, where she teaches poetic theory, literary history, and the social contexts of writing.

Hejinian writes: " 'The Polar Circle' is from a long work entitled *Sleeps*. The initial impetus for *Sleeps* was the *Thousand and One Nights*, from which I extrapolated a notion of my own: to the degree one can say that dreams are an interpretation of waking experience, then by extension one might say that night interprets day—which is, in fact, one of the functions of the tales Scheherazade tells. 'The Polar Circle,' like the other sections of *Sleeps*, is a night work; it was written just after I returned from some weeks spent within the Arctic Circle in Finland and Norway, summer weeks without any night at all (the sun's lower rim would touch the ocean but never sink), and it occurred to me that the poem might serve as a night to that very long day."

ROALD HOFFMANN was born in Zloczow, Poland, in 1937. After escaping from a Nazi labor camp in January 1943, he and his mother hid in the false attic of a Ukrainian schoolhouse, never stepping foot outside until the Soviets arrived in June 1944. The only sunlight came through a hole where a single brick had been removed. He and his mother and stepfather made their way to the United States in 1949. He was educated at Stuyvesant High School in New York City, Columbia, and Harvard, and has taught chemistry at Cornell University since 1965. He was awarded the 1981 Nobel Prize in chemistry for his idea that the ease of chemical transformations could be predicted from the symmetries and asymmetries of electron "orbitals" in complex molecules. The work he did in the mid-1960s with his late mentor, Robert Burns Woodward, proved essential to the synthesis of Vitamin B-12. He lives in Ithaca, New York.

Hoffmann was introduced to poetry by Mark Van Doren at Columbia. His own poems began to appear in the 1980s. Two collections have been published: *The Metamict State* (1987) and *Gaps and Verges* (1990), both from the University of Central Florida Press. "I take some heat from my chemist friends because I write poetry, which they consider just something to do when you're sulking," Hoffmann told Malcolm W. Browne of *The New York Times* (July 6, 1993). "But they should take a look at the respective literatures of chemistry and poetry. The acceptance rate for scientific articles submitted to the best chemical journal in the world is about sixty percent. The acceptance rate for poems sent to even a mediocre poetry journal is about five percent. Furthermore, the poetry editors don't even give you a peer review and critique. They just turn you down flat."

Of "Deceptively Like a Solid," Hoffmann writes: "The poem is about glass, more than you ever wanted to know about glass. It does bring up a problem I face as a chemist who is also a poet. When I write of science, or incorporate scientific language into a poem, there is a terrible pressure I feel—namely, that I must get the science absolutely right. The pressure is self-imposed, I know. But I think the poet who is not a professional scientist will feel it less, for to him or her the license for an occasional transgression is granted. But I sense my scientific colleagues peering over my shoulder.

"I have written a much shorter poem about glass that comple-ments this one. It is called 'Intuition': 'The red-haired woman/ said glass/is tense./She didn't know about disordered /silica chains, rings/and structural/frustration./She just looked/at its fractured/ green/edge.' "

JOHN HOLLANDER was born in New York City in 1929. *A Crackling of Thorns*, his first book of poems, was chosen by W.H. Auden as the 1958 volume in the Yale Series of Younger Poets. Other books include *Types of Shape* (1969), *Reflections on Espionage* (1976), and *Harp Lake* (1988). *Selected Poetry* appeared from Knopf in 1993, as did *Tesserae*, a new collection. Hollander edited the Library of America's two-volume anthology *Nineteenth-Century American Po-etry* (1993). He is A. Bartlett Giamatti Professor of English at Yale University. In *Poetry* (February 1994), Thomas M. Disch remarks that Hollander "has produced, at regular intervals, long lyrical sequences that range in scale from daunting (the seventy-five unrhymed tercets of the dream travelogue, 'The Head of the Bed') to the googolplex lapidary wonders of his 1984 Pelio-on-Ossa special, *Powers of Thirteen*, a work of 169 thirteen-line stanzas, each line being thirteen syllables long."

Of "Variations on a Fragment by Trumbull Stickney," Hollander writes: "The 'fragment' by the fine turn-of-the-century American poet Trumbull Stickney had haunted me for decades; I could never decide whether it was a complete poem or the beginning of an abandoned one. Perhaps it was to have been a villanelle. It kept bothering me, and when I finally laid its ghost in this continuation of it, I kept to the original rhymes in the way of a villanelle, but without the repeated refrains. But it was manifest and latent emblems of time and space, of the heard and the seen, that I was concerned with."

JANET HOLMES was born in Libertyville, Illinois, in 1956, and was educated at Duke University and Warren Wilson College. She grew up in Pompano Beach, Florida, and has lived all over the country, spending the most time in northern New Mexico. There, she edited a weekly newspaper, worked as a technical editor, managed a typesetting operation, and had the occasional adjunct teaching assignment. She now works full-time as program manager for a financial printer in St. Paul, Minnesota, where she lives with her husband, the poet Alvin Greenberg. She has received a Bush Foundation Artist's Fellowship and a Minnesota State Arts Board grant. Her book *The Physicist at the Mall* won the Anhinga Poetry Prize (Anhinga Press, 1994), and a chapbook, *Paperback Romance*, was published by State Street Press in 1984.

Of "The Love of the Flesh," Holmes writes: "The poem began as an elegy for Robert Jebb, founder and editor of Teal Press in Santa Fe, New Mexico. Before he knew he was sick, he introduced me to someone I fell giddily in love with, a feeling I had not expected to have again after the first astonishing times in adolescence. Robert's sudden discovery of his leukemia and his subsequent death both saddened and sobered me while they made me poignantly aware of my present happiness, its likely (and, as it happened, actual) brevity. The poem's original title was 'Elegy and

Prothalamion,' but in revision it became clear that the poem had grown into a more general meditation on body and spirit and the role of each in love. I still associate the poem with Robert.

"During the time the poem was written—and for several years before that—I participated in a weekly Dante reading group headed by the poet and educator Charles Bell. We would translate a canto a week, working through the three books in the archaic Italian and beginning again with *Inferno* when we finished. I came to see those Sunday morning meetings in Charles's house as a family gathering, a strong center to my time in New Mexico. The incident in Paradiso referred to is Dante's conversation with Solomon, in which Dante asks the spirit, who appears as a bright light, whether reclaiming his bodily form at the Last Judgment might be, after Paradise, a bit of a letdown. (Okay, I'm paraphrasing.) Solomon is quick to deny this idea, and all the eavesdropping spirits in the vicinity echo an emphatic 'Amen!': they, too, are eager someday to reinhabit their bodies. Dante gives the lines quoted in the poem as his decorous explanation for their unanimous response. That endorsement of the carnal by the noncorporeal spirits is one of my favorite moments in the *Commedia*."

PAUL HOOVER was born in Harrisonburg, Virginia, in 1946. He now lives in Chicago, where he teaches at Columbia College and edits the literary magazine *New American Writing*. He has published five books of poetry, including the book-length poem *The Novel* (New Directions, 1990). He is the editor of the anthology *Postmodern American Poetry* (Norton, 1994).

Hoover writes: "'Baseball' began with the idea of applying the jargon of feminist studies to the exclusively male activity of professional baseball. At the time of the poem's writing, I was also interested in creating works that relied on their content rather than form; a companion poem, entitled 'Death,' included all that I thought or knew on that subject. The incident at Cincinnati's Crosley Field concerning the man with the gun is reported as it happened. The poem's ending, beginning with Claes Oldenburg's statement about the game's aesthetic qualities, could be taken as my own credo."

RICHARD HOWARD was born in Cleveland, Ohio, in 1929. He has published over one hundred and fifty translations from the French, including Baudelaire's complete *Les Fleurs du mal* (Godine, 1982), for which he received the American Book Award for translation. In 1970 he won the Pulitzer Prize for his third book of poems, *Untitled Subjects* (Atheneum, 1969). Subsequent collections include *Two-Part Inventions* (1974), *Misgivings* (1979), and *Lining Up* (1984), all from Atheneum, and *No Traveller* (Knopf, 1989). His new book of poems is *Like Most Revelations* (Pantheon, 1994), whose title poem appeared in *The Best American Poetry 1992*. At work on a new translation of volume one of Proust's *In Search of Lost Time*, Howard divides his time between Greenwich Village and Texas, where he teaches every fall at the University of Houston.

Of "A Lost Art," Howard writes: "In 1990, I learned of Angelo Solyman's existence in an anniversary account of 'Mozart's Vienna,' marveling that the former's claims to historical attention were both justified and extinguished by the mere fact of having crossed Mozart's path—scarcely a transgression as such things are reckoned. The rest, especially the speaker's nature and the discovery of a particular secret of his art, is a vagary, however adorable, however admonitory."

PHYLLIS JANOWITZ was born in New York City. *Rites of Strangers*, her first book of poems, was chosen by Elizabeth Bishop for the Associated Writing Program's book competition in 1978. She is also the author of *Visiting Rites* (Princeton, 1982) and *Temporary Dwellings* (Pittsburgh, 1988). She has been a Hodder Fellow in the humanities at Princeton and has held two poetry fellowships from the National Endowment for the Arts. She teaches at Cornell University.

Of "The Necessary Angel," Janowitz writes: "What was I thinking when I wrote it? Of course Wallace Stevens's book of essays, *The Necessary Angel*, must have been fluttering in my mind like a piñata. The concept appears in Stevens's poem 'Angel Surrounded by Paysans,' in which he speaks of the 'necessary angel of earth,' who enables the poet to 'see the earth again.' Stevens meant to signify the imagination, while I was thinking more concretely of a woman: a muse, an artist, a poet, a performer, even perhaps a financial backer for a play, or my mother visiting school during 'open school week'—a working woman dressed in a suit and rose-blue hat. Elegant."

MARK JARMAN was born in Mt. Sterling, Kentucky, in 1952. He is a professor of English at Vanderbilt University in Nashville, Tennessee. He has published five books of poetry: *North Sea* (Cleveland State University Poetry Center, 1978), *The Rote Walker* (Carnegie-Mellon University Press, 1981), *Far and Away* (Carnegie-Mellon, 1985), *The Black Riviera* (Wesleyan University Press, 1990), and *Iris*, a book-length poem (Story Line Press, 1992). David R. Godine will publish his sixth book, *Questions for Ecclesiastes*, in 1995. *The Black Riviera* won The Poets' Prize for 1991.

Jarman writes: "John Donne's *Holy Sonnets* are the models for my Unholy Sonnets. His poems are urgent declarations of faith and appeals for mercy, despite the obvious realities of sin and death. Donne applies terrific pressure to form and metaphor, and both at times come close to collapse. Still, he works from Anglo-Catholic, Christian assumptions widely disseminated and shared in his time. It is almost impossible to work from such assumptions today. My aim was to work against any assumption or shared expression of faith, to write a devotional poetry against the grain. At the same time I wanted to write traditional sonnets, but did not want to stick to any one traditional form. So the Unholy Sonnets (there are over twenty) include English, Italian, Spenserian, composite, and nonce forms. Calling them Unholy is a way of warding off piety but not, I hope, ultimately, belief."

ALICE JONES was born in Cincinnati in 1949. A psychiatrist in the San Francisco Bay area, she is a graduate of Goddard College and New York Medical College. She did her residency in internal medicine at a county hospital, Highland General in Oakland, and her residency in psychiatry at the Langley Porter Psychiatric Institute of the University of California at San Francisco. Her book *The Knot* won the Beatrice Hawley Award. She received a poetry fellowship from the National Endowment for the Arts in 1994.

Jones writes: " 'The Foot' is one of a series of poems about parts of the body, from an unpublished chapbook manuscript. I wrote the series as I was working on a long poem, 'The Cadaver,' to balance its heaviness with lightness, its length with brevity. In form, each poem in the group suggests something of the organ's structure: 'The Heart' is in long-short couplets, 'The Larynx' is written in one breathless sentence, 'The Foot' is in five stubby stanzas.

"After medical school, I did a residency in and practiced internal medicine. Later I did a second residency in psychiatry, and now practice psychoanalysis in Oakland. I think poetry remains centered in the body, as do the most useful of psychological theories. I can't read poems without becoming conscious of breath, voice, diaphragm, the body's resonance feeding the poem. This series of body poems is part of my effort to fuse my two worlds. Besides, after spending years learning this rich vocabulary, I didn't want to abandon it."

RODNEY JONES was born in Hartselle, Alabama, in 1950. His books include *Apocalyptic Narrative and Other Poems* (Houghton Mifflin, 1993), *Transparent Gestures* (Houghton Mifflin, 1989), and *The Unborn* (Atlantic Monthly Press, 1985). He has received grants from the Guggenheim Foundation and the National Endowment for the Arts, as well as the Jean Stein Award from the American Academy of Arts and Letters and the 1989 National Book Critics Circle Award for poetry. He teaches at Southern Illinois University at Carbondale.

Of "Contempt," Jones writes: "I had just read Seneca's 'On Contempt,' which must be one of the sanest essays ever written on political correctness. According to Seneca, it is inappropriate for a person in a position of power to express contempt for a subordinate, but altogether appropriate, even admirable, for subordinates to express contempt for those in power. Clearly, the master can take a good roasting; Shakespeare's fools get the best put-downs; the betrayed have the last word in love. This is doubtless all for the best, a civilizing impulse of our essential simian nature. Nevertheless, I have always felt partial to those few souls rowdy enough to express contempt of sufficient magnitude to defy any possible exemptions. Such heroic contempt suggests a kind of affectionate trust, and I much prefer it to more popular expressions such as pity and violence. The focal character in my meditative narrative is one of these characters. 'Lizards,' he says, meaning you, me, the world. I can only add that the events and characters of the poem obviously bear some relation to my brief experience writing advertisements and technical articles in the poultry industry. Those women in that processing plant really did cackle at me and my friend, and surely they had the right. Their jobs were even worse than ours, and they had no way of knowing that they were poking at the ashes of Rimbaud and Verlaine."

BRIGIT PEGEEN KELLY was born in Palo Alto, California, in 1951. She has received the Nation/Discovery Award, the Yale Younger Poets Prize, and a National Endowment for the Arts fellowship. *To the Place of Trumpets*, her first book, was published by Yale University Press in 1988. She teaches creative writing at the University of Illinois at Champaign-Urbana.

Kelly writes: " 'Courting the Famous Figures at the Grotto of Improbable Thought' was written for my friend Julia Fogarty. The first line of the poem is derived from the following passage in Edmund G. Gardner's book *The King of Court Poets: A Study of the Work and Times of Lodovico Ariosto*: 'On the curtain was painted the Pope's Dominican jester or buffoon, Fra Mariano, sporting with devils, with the inscription: *Questi sono li capricci di Fra Mariano*: These are the japeries of Fra Mariano.' "

CAROLINE KNOX was born in Boston in 1938. She was educated at Radcliffe College and the University of Wisconsin, Milwaukee. Her books are *The House Party* (1984) and *To Newfoundland* (1989), both from Georgia. A third collection, *Sleepers Wake*, will appear from Timken Publishers in 1994. An assistant professor of English at the University of Connecticut at Avery Point (Groton), she lives in Rhode Island.

Knox writes: "In 'A Rune,' I wanted to make a prose poem about the size and shape of what its I-narrator might be 'thinking' while reluctantly mowing the lawn. The poem was supposed to include lots of dull jokes for the dull occupation. The voice was supposed to change diction levels and syntax constantly, listening to itself."

KENNETH KOCH was born in Cincinnati, Ohio, in 1925. He lives in New York City and teaches at Columbia University. His recent books include *One Thousand Avant-Garde Plays* (Knopf, 1988), *Seasons on Earth* (Viking, 1987), *On the Edge* (Viking, 1986), and *Selected Poems* (Random House, 1985). An operatic version of his play "The Construction of Boston," with music by Scott Wheeler, was produced in Boston in 1989 and 1990. *Hotel Lambosa*, a book of stories, appeared from Coffee House Press in 1993. In 1994 Knopf will publish *One Train*, a book of new poems, and *On the Great Atlantic Rainway*, a new edition of selected poems.

Of "One Train May Hide Another," Koch writes: "I saw the railway-crossing sign 'one train may hide another' when I was traveling in Africa in 1982. I wrote it down in a journal I was keeping and thought about it from time to time till a few years ago, when I finally wrote a poem about it. Apparently, there are quite a few signs of this kind, in Kenya, England, and elsewhere. In France, too, where what they say is '*un train peut en cacher un autre.*'"

DIONISIO D. MARTÍNEZ was born in Cuba in 1956 and has lived in exile since 1965. In 1993 he was the recipient of a Whiting Writers' Award from the Whiting Foundation, a James Wright Poetry Prize from *Mid-American Review*, and an Emerging Artist Grant from the Arts Council of Hillsborough County, Florida. His poetry collections include *Bad Alchemy* (forthcoming from Norton), *History as a Second Language* (Ohio State, 1993 [winner of the 1992 Ohio State University Press/*The Journal* Poetry Award]), and *Dancing at the Chelsea* (State Street Chapbooks, 1992). He lives in Tampa, Florida, and works as a poet in the schools. His work was included in *The Best American Poetry 1992*.

Martínez writes: "'Avant-Dernières Pensées' ('Next-to-Last Thoughts') is the title of a piano composition by Erik Satie. This poem is part of a sequence. Like the other eight poems in the group, it was *not* written as an interpretation of Satie's music: that would have been a pointless exercise. The idea here was to work with whatever impression the music left in me. For years I've been fascinated and seduced by the works of the French composer. Something childlike and terribly frightening (children often have great fears) is always happening in Satie's music. The high notes sound as though they're coming from a toy, but I never know where they're headed. Perhaps the music is unaware of its own destination. Such exquisite abandon! What I wanted for my Satie poems was much simpler: imagine balls of yarn unraveling in a landscape of their own making, like cartographers with a poor sense of direction."

J. D. MCCLATCHY was born in Bryn Mawr, Pennsylvania, in 1945, and now lives in Stonington, Connecticut. He has taught at Yale, Princeton, U.C.L.A., and other universities, and currently serves as editor of *The Yale Review*. Three collections of his poems have been published: *Scenes from Another Life* (Braziller, 1981), *Stars Principal* (Macmillan, 1986), and *The Rest of the Way* (Knopf, 1990). He has also written opera libretti, edited several books, and gathered his essays in *White Paper* (Columbia University Press, 1989). He has received an award from the American Academy of Arts and Letters and fellowships from the Guggenheim Foundation and the National Endowment for the Arts.

Of "Found Parable," McClatchy writes: "A lot of the best thinking I do—you, too?—happens in what the Victorians primly referred to as the smallest room in the house. Both my pants and my guard are down, and there's no telephone.

"Why, I wonder now, did I give this toilet-trained poem the title it bears? It's meant, I suspect, sheepishly to insist on the poem's 'naturalism'—as if I'd merely overheard what Wordsworth would call a sermon in stone. But what we find, and what we make of it, are very different matters indeed. So the title clears its throat to announce a doubled ambition: an artless subject simply come upon, and a moral shape given to the materials of that subject.

"(For the record, a few years ago in the Princeton University Arts Building, where I had an office, I did one morning encounter the drawing and graffiti I describe verbatim in the poem. As soon as I returned to my office, I jotted down the sequence in a notebook, and a few days later set about turning the remarks into literature. I first wrote it out as prose; for two years it sat in a workbook until I decided to revise and lineate it.)

"How often, in fact *do* poems just offer themselves—unbidden and complete—to a writer? Less often, of course, than we want to believe. What we *want* to believe is what we've been taught by Romantics from Keats to Freud: to prefer the spontaneous, the primitive, the instinctual, and to distrust the deliberate, the retouched, the overwrought. Our art must come as easily as leaves to a tree or it had better not come at all. But art is all will, however nature or the imagination may conjure its subjects.

"Besides, in this particular poem, I was fascinated by the contrast between high and low, natural and artificial. The relationship between sex and thought works both ways. Our erotic lives are two-thirds *idea*. And Auden reminded us of 'the foiled caresses from which thought was born.' This poem's energies should be generated for a reader by the tension between the immoral pleasures of pornography and the moral purposes of parable: graffiti-as-commentary, smut and its metaphysical discontents, art and eros and the Higher Criticisms.

"The koan-like last sentence of the poem is by way of Wittgenstein.

"'Found Parable' is actually part of a long sequence-in-progress that broods on the Ten Commandments. It will eventually be filed under False Gods."

JEFFREY MCDANIEL was born in Philadelphia in 1967. He graduated from Sarah Lawrence College. In 1993 he represented Washington, D.C., in the national poetry slam. He edited *Phoebe* from fall 1991 to spring 1993. He is the poetry editor of *Hyper Age*. He has a manuscript, *House of Separate Beds*. He is editing a book of interviews, each about one specific poem, *Anatomy of a Poem*.

Of "Following Her to Sleep," McDaniel writes: "I visited a woman in Colorado, and we were both keeping secrets, which made the trip a disaster but helped generate the poem."

JAMES MCMANUS was born in the Bronx in 1951. His poems have appeared in the *Atlantic Monthly*, *New American Writing*, *Parnassus*, *American Poetry Review*, *Honest Ulsterman*, *Harvard Magazine*, and *The Best American Poetry 1991*. He has received prizes and fellowships from Arts International, the Shifting Foundation, and the National Endowment for the Arts. His novels are *Out of the Blue* (1983), *Chin Music* (1985), and *Ghost Waves* (1988), all from Grove Press. *Great America*, his first collection of poems, was published in 1993 by HarperCollins. He was awarded a Guggenheim Fellowship in poetry in 1994. He teaches at The School of the Art Institute of Chicago.

Of "Spike Logic," McManus writes: "The speaker of this poem is enraged. He has to stab himself with needles and triphammer lancets seven or eight times a day in order to provide his system with insulin and monitor his blood sugar levels, yet he keeps getting sicker. The incessant requirement that he puncture himself has generated a kind of deranged, lucid 'spike logic.' (The horseshoe-shaped conditional in line three means 'implies' or 'if . . . then.' The sense of the line is therefore: 'if my sugar is 166 then I give myself 34 units of Regular . . .') Spike logic is the clinically straightforward logic of the management of his disease, but it's also the jagged, out-of-control way his brain works when he's obsessed or pissed off. And he's both. His fifteen early-morning quatrains are barely able to contain his headlong, sarcastic, ungenerous, self-interrupting, metrically schizoid, often not parallel tirade. Sometimes they rhyme *abab* rather suavely, sometimes *aabb* or *abba* or *xaax*, sometimes they don't rhyme at all. The thing is, he could probably make each of them rhyme in one of the various classical manners—he's tempted to more than a little—but he flagrantly refuses. (He'd much rather mock-rhyme, say, 'ball' with 'testicle,' '-yo' with '*yo!?*,' or drag out a line just to match 'get a' with 'vulva,' leaving 'hardon' enjambed between them but more or less out of the picture. It's one of the ways he gets even.) He's also, whether he admits it or not, in a distinctly 'Ash Wednesday,' 'East Coker' sort of mood: he's scared, so he's praying for help."

JAMES MERRILL was born in New York City in 1926. He received his B.A. from Amherst College in 1947 and published his *First Poems* in 1951. His books have received two National Book Awards, the Pulitzer Prize, and the Bollingen Prize. The epic poem begun in *Divine Comedies* (1976) and extended in two subsequent volumes was published in its entirety as *The Changing Light at Sandover* (1983), which won the National Book Critics Circle Award. His most recent books of poetry are *Late Settings* (Atheneum, 1985) and *The Inner Room* (Knopf, 1988). *A Different Person*, a memoir about the years he spent in Europe in the early 1950s, appeared from Knopf in 1993. He divides his time between Stonington, Connecticut, and Key West, Florida.

Merrill writes that "Family Week at Oracle Ranch" is "all fairly straightforward, although the name of the institution has been changed."

W. S. MERWIN was born in New York City in 1927, and grew up in Union City, New Jersey, and in Scranton, Pennsylvania. From 1949 to 1951 he worked as a tutor in France, Portugal, and Majorca, and later earned his living by translating from the French, Spanish, Latin, and Portuguese. He has also lived in England and in Mexico. *A Mask for Janus*, his first book of poems, was chosen by W. H. Auden as the 1952 volume in the Yale Series of Younger Poets. Subsequent volumes include *The Moving Target* (1963), *The Compass Flower* (1977), and *The Rain in the Trees* (Knopf, 1988). *The Carrier of Ladders* (1970) won the Pulitzer Prize. He has translated *The Poem of the Cid* and *The Song of Roland*, and his *Selected Translations 1948–1968* won the P.E.N. Translation Prize for 1968. In 1987 he received the Governor's Award for Literature of the State of

Hawaii. *Travels*, his latest collection of poems, appeared from Knopf in 1993. Other recent books are *The Lost Upland* (1992, Knopf), about France, and *The Second Four Books* (Copper Canyon, 1993), poems. He lives in Hawaii—in a place called Haiku, on the island of Maui.

Merwin notes that "One of the Lives" is "one of an as yet unfinished series" of poems.

STEPHEN PAUL MILLER was born on Staten Island, New York, in 1951. He is an assistant professor of English at St. John's University in New York City, and is currently writing a book about American culture of the 1970s for Duke University Press. His plays have been performed in New York, San Francisco, and the University of Vermont. He has written several books of poetry including *That Man Who Ground Moths into Film* (New Observations, 1982), *Doctor Shy* (New Observations, 1983), and *Art Is Boring for the Same Reason We Stayed in Vietnam* (The Domestic Press, 1992).

Of "I Was on a Golf Course the Day John Cage Died of a Stroke," Miller writes: "I wrote the poem upon hearing of John Cage's death. I used what was immediate to me that day to evoke the John Cage I knew, his supreme magnanimity and dedication to an art that bypasses ego and intention so as to perceive the everyday. I would like to apply his aesthetic to my own concerns of discourse and social impact."

JENNY MUELLER was born in Lake Forest, Illinois, in 1962. She received her B.A. and M.A. degrees from the University of Chicago and was a teaching fellow at the University of Iowa Writers' Workshop from 1990 until 1992. She has worked as an arts administrator in Boston, and now lives in Chicago.

Of "Allegory," Mueller writes: "When I wrote this poem I told my friends at the Iowa Writers' Workshop that my mother (the poet Lisel Mueller) could have written it blindfolded with her hands tied behind her back. It's the poem of mine that most closely resembles her work."

HARRYETTE MULLEN was born, like W.C. Handy, in Florence, Alabama. She grew up in Fort Worth, Texas, home of Ornette Coleman. She graduated with honors from the University of Texas at

Austin and has graduate degrees from the University of California, Santa Cruz. Her books include *S*PeRM**K*T* (Singing Horse Press, 1992), *Trimmings* (Tender Button Press, 1991), and *Tree Tall Woman* (Energy Earth Communications, 1981). She lives in Ithaca, New York, and teaches at Cornell University.

Mullen writes: "*Muse & Drudge* is a praise-song to the women of Africa, to their daughters and sisters of the diaspora. It is also dedicated to blues men, poets and singers, who are fond of saying, 'If it wasn't for women, we wouldn't have the blues.' *Muse & Drudge*, a book-length work in progress, is a return to verse after two books of prose poetry. For me it marks a crossroads where Sappho meets the blues lyric. My poetry would not be here if not for some praiseworthy people. I thank them: A. R. Ammons and Stephen Yenser, for unbounded generosity. Thomas Sayers Ellis, of the Dark Room Collective, for choosing to excerpt *Muse & Drudge* in *Agni Review* and *Muleteeth*. Leslie Scalapino, whose Boston poetry reading, among other delights, allowed me to meet Tom Ellis, Barbara Henning, and David St. John, who have encouraged me by publishing parts of the poem. Diane Rayor, whose American language translations of Sappho and other divine dead Greeks reminded me so much of the blues, I couldn't wait to start a new poem in verse. Gwendolyn Brooks, pathbreaker. Ted Pearson, the most lyrical poet alive. For what they have given, I praise them!"

BRIGHDE MULLINS was born in 1964 in Camp LeJeune, North Carolina, and grew up in Las Vegas, Nevada. She attended Yale University, the University of Iowa, and Columbia University. She is the author of eight plays and two opera libretti. Her work has been produced Off-Broadway at La Mama ETC, the Ensemble Studio Theatre, and the Women's Project. In 1990 she was a Eugene O'Neill Fellow, and in 1992 she received a fellowship in playwriting from the National Endowment for the Arts. She is the director of arts education and poetry at the Dia Center for the Arts in New York City.

Of "At the Lakehouse," Mullins writes: "'At the Lakehouse' is one in a long line of elegies I've been writing for the living and the dead. I wanted the clarification in the tenth stanza to occur in the way that shifts occur in one's visual field, while one is walking and naming objects, or the way realizations occur in the theater, when a relationship or a motive becomes—for a brief instant—intelligible, lucid. I was reading Henry James at the time, and there are some Jamesian constructions in the poem."

FRED MURATORI was born in Connecticut in 1951, and holds degrees from Fairfield and Syracuse universities. In 1990 he was awarded an artist's fellowship in poetry from the New York Foundation for the Arts. A chapbook of poems, *The Possible*, was published by State Street Press in 1988. *Despite Repeated Warnings*, a full-length collection, is scheduled for spring 1994 publication by BASFAL Books. His reviews of current poetry appear regularly in *Library Journal* and sporadically elsewhere. He is employed as a reference librarian and lives in Dryden, New York.

Muratori writes: " 'Sensible Qualities' takes its title from the philosophy of George Berkeley, who used the term to denote those characteristics by which things are perceived or perceivable. The poem is from *The Spectra*, a manuscript of fifteen-line meditative lyrics largely concerned with the frustrations inherent in experiencing and comprehending an overbrimming world constricted only by our own malevolent consciousness of time. They attempt at once to be abstract and imagistic, vortical, rhetorical, and more than a little rushed in their sometimes self-contradictory conclusions, like ancient seafarers swept irrevocably toward the earth's edge, warning the rest of us away long after it's too late."

SHARON OLDS was born in San Francisco in 1942. Her books are *Satan Says* (University of Pittsburgh Press, 1980); and *The Dead and the Living* (1984), *The Gold Cell* (1987), and *The Father* (1992), all published by Knopf. She teaches in the graduate creative writing program at New York University, and, with N.Y.U. writing students, at Goldwater Hospital, a nine-hundred-bed New York public hospital for the severely physically disabled. She received a three-year writer's award from the Lila Wallace–Reader's Digest Fund in 1992.

Of "The Knowing," Olds writes: "I remember that, as I was writing this poem, it felt very simple, uncomplex, very plain, just 1, 2, 3—or A, B, C, D—step by step, one foot in front of the other. (Later, I was surprised I had not written it sooner—but probably there are things so close to one's eyes that it takes a long time to see them.) I felt sad, a little, as well as happy, that the poem had sort of written itself, that it had not needed me to *work*, or *craft*, but just to stand out of the way as much as possible."

MAUREEN OWEN was born in Graceville, Minnesota, in 1943. She lived in Japan for several years and began publishing *Telephone* magazine in New York City in 1969. For a number of years she was program coordinator at the Poetry Project of St. Mark's Church in New York. Her recent books include *Imaginary Income* (Hanging Loose Press, 1992) and *Untapped Maps* (Potes & Poets Press, 1993). She lives in Connecticut with her three sons and is catalogue manager for the Inland Book Company in East Haven.

Of "Them," Owen writes: "Though in its abstraction the poem takes on a wider range of possibilities, originally it was a description of two odd characters I came to refer to as 'the housemates from Hell.' My work tends to come out of screaming real life and I am a big fan of description. This poem became for me a kind of exorcism, a way to deal with these two characters."

KATHLEEN PEIRCE was born in Moline, Illinois, in 1956. She teaches in the M.F.A. program at Southwest Texas State University. *Mercy*, her first book, won the 1990 AWP Award in poetry and was published by the University of Pittsburgh Press. A chapbook, *Divided Touch, Divided Color*, will appear from Windhover Press. She received a 1993 Whiting Writers' Award.

Of "Divided Touch, Divided Color," Peirce writes: "I had been studying a book of Seurat's paintings and found myself disturbed by and drawn to the pointillist method, by which the world is assembled with such tense precision that it is inevitably fragile, frighteningly so, regardless of the heft of the image seen from a distance. I looked up from *Young Woman Powdering Herself* and saw the rain in the yew outside my house, and the berries; and the poem began. Parts of the poem are biographical: Seurat's father did juggle the knives, and Paul Signac described Seurat's method as 'divided touch, divided color.' "

CARL PHILLIPS was born in Everett, Washington, in 1959, and grew up on air force bases. He was a classics major at Harvard. He taught Latin for nearly ten years before attending the writing program at Boston University as the George Starbuck Fellow. He has been awarded a Massachusetts Artists Foundation fellowship and the

Academy of American Poets Prize. His first collection, *In the Blood* (Northeastern University Press, 1992), won the Samuel French Morse poetry prize. Teaching in both the English and African-American Studies departments he is now poet-in-residence at Washington University in St. Louis.

Of "A Mathematics of Breathing," Phillips writes: "The poem arose from a rather sudden chain of events, the end result of which was that I knew that my life as I'd known it had passed, along with—perhaps more important—the knowledge of how to live any kind of a life. In the effort to recover this knowledge, it seemed important to examine even the least noticed, most taken-for-granted parts of a life—breathing, for example. To understand human breathing, it became necessary to know what nonhuman breathing, if it existed, might be. I had in mind, too, that if such things as buildings and bushes could be made to breathe, so could the most ruined or seemingly ruined lives. It was in this time of reconstruction that the poem found its own construction."

LLOYD SCHWARTZ was born in Brooklyn, New York, in 1941. He teaches at the University of Massachusetts in Boston, where he is co-director of the creative writing program. He is also both the classical music editor and the poetry editor of the *Boston Phoenix* and the commentator on classical music for National Public Radio's "Fresh Air." He is the author of two books of poetry, *These People* (Wesleyan Poetry Series, 1981) and *Goodnight, Gracie* (University of Chicago Press, 1992), and co-editor of *Elizabeth Bishop and Her Art* (University of Michigan Press, 1983). His writing on the arts has appeared in *Vanity Fair*, *Atlantic Monthly*, and *The New Yorker*. He has received an NEA Creative Writing Fellowship Grant for his poetry and three ASCAP–Deems Taylor Awards for his music criticism. He won the Pulitzer Prize in 1994 for his "skillful and resonant" criticism.

"Pornography," Schwartz writes, "is under fire not only from the conservative right but also from the politically correct left. I've always found it fascinating—more often for what it reveals about the participants themselves than for its ability to stimulate the libido (although I'm not puritanical about the latter, either). When a friend of mine, a scholar of noncanonical nineteenth-century Americana, acquired an extensive collection of nineteenth- and early-twentieth-century 'French postcards,' I was invited to look them over. Three of the images first touched and then haunted me. The figures seemed so convincing in their pleasure, yet so vulnerable. I couldn't get them out of my head. This was the last subject I expected to write a poem about. The year I won an NEA grant, I had to promise not to use it to 'promote, disseminate, or produce materials . . . which, when taken as a whole, do not have serious literary, artistic, political, or scientific value.' Although the poem was published several years after I made this promise, it remains my sincerest intention to comply with this stipulation—in all four categories."

FREDERICK SEIDEL was born in St. Louis in 1936, attended Harvard College, and now lives in New York City. In 1980 his book *Sunrise* won the National Book Critics Circle Award for poetry. *Poems 1959–1979* and *These Days* appeared from Knopf in 1989. *My Tokyo*, his latest book, was published by Farrar, Straus & Giroux in 1993, the year he received a Guggenheim Fellowship.

ALAN SHAPIRO was born in Boston in 1952. He received his B.A. from Brandeis University in 1974. He has published four books of poetry: *After the Digging* (Elpenor Books, 1981); *The Courtesy* (University of Chicago Press, 1983); *Happy Hour* (University of Chicago Press, 1987); and *Covenant* (University of Chicago Press, 1991). His most recent book, *In Praise of the Impure: Poetry and the Ethical Imagination, Essays 1980–1991*, was published in 1993 by TriQuarterly Books, an imprint of Northwestern University Press. He has received fellowships from the National Endowment for the Arts and the Guggenheim Foundation. He was a 1991 recipient of a Lila Wallace–Reader's Digest Fund writer's award. A professor of English and creative writing at the University of North Carolina, Greensboro, he lives in Chapel Hill, North Carolina, with his wife and two children.

Shapiro writes: " 'The Letter' is partly a retelling, in reverse, of the Orpheus/Eurydice myth. In the original story, the male lover leads his beloved up out of the underworld, and the beloved vanishes when he turns around; in my version, the beloved leads the speaker down into the underworld and makes him vanish when she turns away. Beyond this, I think the poem expresses both the dangers and attractions implicit in a certain kind of longing."

ANGELA SHAW was born in Denville, New Jersey, in 1967, and grew up in the mountains of West Virginia. She graduated from Swarthmore College and is a student in the M.F.A. program at Cornell University.

Shaw writes: "I wrote 'Courtesan' in the spring of 1993. I had been reading about corsets and thinking about washing dishes. What interests me about this speaker is her awareness of the disjunction between her public and private selves, her knowledge of what is lost to an audience and of what may be regained through solitude."

CHARLES SIMIC was born in Belgrade, Yugoslavia, in 1938, came to the United States at the age of sixteen, went to high school in Oak Park, Illinois, and attended New York University. His first volume of poetry was published in 1967. Fifteen others have followed. He received the Pulitzer Prize in 1990 for his book of prose poems, *The World Doesn't End*. His most recent collections are *The Book of Gods and Devils* (1990) and *Hotel Insomnia* (1992), both from Harcourt Brace. In 1992 he published two books of translations—Novica Tadic's *Night Mail: Selected Poems* (Oberlin College Press) and *The Horse Has Six Legs: An Anthology of Serbian Poetry* (Graywolf)—as well as a book of musings on the art of Joseph Cornell, *Dime-Store Alchemy* (Ecco). He was guest editor of *The Best American Poetry 1992*. Awarded a MacArthur Fellowship in 1984, Simic teaches at the University of New Hampshire.

Of "Read Your Fate," Simic writes: "The original title was 'Where Dreamy Wabash Flows.' The poem just took off from a few initial images in a direction that is as mysterious to me as it must be to the reader."

W. D. SNODGRASS was born in Wilkinsburg, Pennsylvania, in 1926. He attended Geneva College and served in the navy during World War II. He was a member of the legendary entering class of 1953 at the University of Iowa Writers' Workshop. (His classmates included Donald Justice, Philip Levine, Henri Coulette, and Jane Cooper; among their instructors were Robert Lowell and John Berryman.) *Heart's Needle*, his first book, won the Pulitzer Prize for poetry in 1960. *Selected Poems 1957–1987* appeared in 1987 (SoHo Press). *Each in His Season*, his most recent collection, was published in 1993 by BOA Publications in Brockport, New York. He has taught for many years at the University of Delaware.

Snodgrass writes: " 'Snow Songs' is part of a cycle, *Each in His Season*, which gives its title to my most recent book. I began these poems in San Miguel de Allende, Mexico, after hearing the pianist Walter Ponce play a set of theme and variations by Beethoven. Wanting to try such a group, and feeling rather autumnal, I did the first cycle, *Autumn Variations*. Having finished these, I decided to go on and do a cycle of eight or ten short poems for each season. 'Snow Songs' was the second of these. I called the complete work *Each in His Season* because I already have a book entitled *The Four Seasons*—translations of the four Italian sonnets that accompany Vivaldi's famous concerti—a beautiful edition complete with quotations from the concerti and issued by William Targ Publications, New York City."

ELIZABETH SPIRES was born in Lancaster, Ohio, in 1952 and grew up in nearby Circleville. Her books of poems are *Globe* (Wesleyan 1981), *Swan's Island* (Holt, 1985), and *Annonciade* (Viking Penguin, 1989). She lives in Baltimore and teaches in the Writing Seminars at Johns Hopkins University and in the English Department at Goucher College. Her work has appeared in four previous editions of *The Best American Poetry*. A recent Guggenheim Fellow, she is completing a new manuscript of poems and has a book of riddles for children forthcoming from Margaret McElderry Books.

Spires writes: " 'The Robed Heart' is one of a group of poems centered on the conception, birth, and infancy of my daughter Celia. While some of the other poems take a more literal, autobiographical approach to the subject of childbirth and motherhood, 'The Robed Heart' presented itself to me as an allegorical image such as one might find in a medieval illumination. The poem is one of the shortest I've ever written."

A. E. STALLINGS was born in Champaign, Illinois, in 1968, and grew up in Atlanta, Georgia, where she still lives. She studied classics, first at the University of Georgia, and later at Oxford University. Currently a secretary at Georgia State University, she is working on a novel. She is seeking a publisher for her first collection of poems, *Love Poems from the Institute of Classical Studies*.

Of "Apollo Takes Charge of His Muses," Stallings writes: "Typical, isn't it, that nine goddesses of creativity couldn't be allowed to wander the Universe unchaperoned. Eventually the god Apollo was put in charge of them. I like picturing this gradual conceptual shift as an actual event. If I am a bit free with classical tradition, well, I do so on the precedent of the ancients themselves. Like the ancients, I enjoy pirating mythology for my own purposes, and juxtaposing the fabulous with the mundane."

MARK STRAND was born in Canada of American parents in 1934. After many years of teaching at the University of Utah in Salt Lake City, he now lives in Baltimore and teaches in the Writing Seminars at Johns Hopkins University. He has held a MacArthur Foundation Fellowship. He is the author of nine books of poetry, all of them either published or reissued by Knopf. His most recent books are *Dark Harbor* (1993) and *The Continuous Life* (1990). He was guest editor of *The Best American Poetry 1991*, which he worked on during his tenure as the nation's fourth poet laureate, in 1990–91.

Of "The Mysterious Maps," Mark Strand writes: "I sent *The New Yorker* the forty-five sections of *Dark Harbor*, giving them first crack at it. They picked twelve sections, but I didn't want the sections to be published individually. I figured that four groups of three might work best, and so did they. Alice Quinn and Chip McGrath did the groupings, and 'The Mysterious Maps' is one of the groups. So I have Alice and Chip to thank for its final form."

SHARAN STRANGE was born in Heidelberg, Germany, in 1959 and grew up in Orangeburg, South Carolina. She was educated at Harvard and at Sarah Lawrence, where she is currently pursuing the M.F.A. in creative writing. She is a founding member of the Dark Room Collective, a group of emerging African-American writers who run the Dark Room Reading Series at the Boston University Playwrights' Theatre. She has had residencies at Yaddo and the MacDowell Colony. Her writings have appeared in *Agni Review*, *Callaloo*, *Eyeball*, *In the Tradition*, *Muleteeth*, and *Racism Defined*.

Strange writes: " 'Offering' attempts to address, in a small way, my father's death and my 'unresolved' relationship with him. The imagery came from a series of dreams I've had over the years since his death (on August 28, 1983, the weekend I was attending the

Twentieth Anniversary March on Washington). My father did not encourage me to write or to dream, but he was a strong presence in my life in many ways, not all of them bad (I am beginning to realize and understand some of this). So the poem attempts to capture that, and the sense of loss, the chasm his death made, and the impossibility of a mutual resolution of our afflicted relationship. My childhood/memory poems are a kind of telescoping view of my life. Here, another lens—that of dream: the meaning the unconscious holds . . . the notion of recurrence, and, therefore, of possibility, of hope . . . I am particularly gratified that the poem was first published in *Callaloo* and appears here via its auspices. It seems a fitting culmination of my efforts, the Dark Room's nurturance, and Charles Rowell's 'hospitality' to us 'new jacks.' "

MAY SWENSON (1913–1989) was born in Logan, Utah. Her books include *A Cage of Spines* (1958), *Half Sun Half Sleep* (Scribners, 1967), and *In Other Words* (Knopf, 1987). She translated from the Swedish the selected poems of Tomas Tranströmer, *Windows and Stones* (University of Pittsburgh Press, 1972). She received many honors and awards, including Rockefeller and Guggenheim grants, the Bollingen Prize, and a MacArthur Fellowship. Three books of her poetry have been posthumously published: *The Love Poems of May Swenson* (Houghton Mifflin, 1991), *The Complete Poems to Solve* (Macmillan, 1993), and *Nature* (Houghton Mifflin, 1994). Her correspondence with Elizabeth Bishop would fill a five-hundred-page book that many readers would welcome; a selection will appear in a forthcoming issue of *The Paris Review*. "Sleeping with Boa" was written on November 28, 1980, and left unpublished at the time of her death on December 4, 1989.

In a letter to Elizabeth Bishop written on June 24, 1958, May Swenson wrote: "From the beginning I came to poetry backwards. I never acquired a background in what had already been done by others. . . . To date I've never followed a pre-determined form, either one of my own or in imitation of others. . . . I try to impose consistency and an inner logic for each poem—but a *total* consistency or a pre-arranged logic or following a strict form, that doesn't work for me—I don't *enjoy* that. . . . The poems I think are worth something (a few) have *come* to me from somewhere—it hardly feels as though I made them."

JANET SYLVESTER was born in Youngstown, Ohio, in 1950. She received her B.A. and M.F.A. degrees from Goddard College in Vermont and her Ph.D. from the University of Utah. Her first book, *That Mulberry Wine*, was published by Wesleyan University Press. "Modern Times" appears in the manuscript of her second book, *Regardless*, which has not yet been published. She lives in Norfolk, Virginia, and teaches at Old Dominion University.

Of "Modern Times," Sylvester writes: "I am teaching Dante again in a craft-of-poetry class. As usual when I do this, everything in my world exists in reference to Dante's poem, which I use to teach metaphor by proposing, among other things, that the *Comedy* is a metaphor for the way in which any poem gets made. We begin by talking about how a momentary vision calls forth the necessity of a poem. So I apologize for the consequent analogy, which opens when Jonathan called me from New York on Memorial Day in 1989. Believe me, I had none of these things in mind then. My memory of his compassion, though, is vivid: how he asked me to sit down; how he told me that our mutual friend of twenty years (and my first great love) had died of AIDS; how he waited patiently for an amount of time I still can't determine, while I stared speechlessly out my window at a long valley surrounded by mountains; how he told me that Bill had asked continually for me, though he could no longer remember where I had gone; how he listened to the long-distance weeping, which he assured me was nothing new for him anymore. For a moment, I knew something that eludes me now, as I try to write here, but occurs, I hope, in the course of the poem—that life is excess, fragile in its repetitiveness, and that love, the shock of its durability, can render life insupportably beautiful. But you know this. Maybe all that I meant to say is, 'I'm with you. I'm here.'"

JAMES TATE was born in Kansas City, Missouri, in 1943. He was awarded the Yale Younger Poets Prize in 1966 for *The Lost Pilot*. His *Selected Poems* (Wesleyan/University Press of New England, 1991) was awarded the Pulitzer Prize for poetry in 1992. Other recent books include *Reckoner* (Wesleyan University Press, 1986), *Distance from Loved Ones* (Wesleyan/University Press of New England, 1990), and *Worshipful Company of Fletchers* (Ecco Press, 1994). He teaches at the University of Massachusetts and lives in Amherst.

Of "Like a Scarf," Tate writes: "I had fun writing this poem. I guess the subtext has to do with our relationship to language: when we think we're sane and even powerful our diction and syntax can inflate. And then there's the change in the poem when power ebbs away from the speaker, and he ends with near-nonsense. Inflation and deflation, power and the loss of it. Language drifting away, becoming private, not public.

"And then, also, there's the little matter of making a 'narrative' out of nothing, which is surely an activity we pursue much of our lives, the promise of continuity, of flow, when it's often just so much flotsam and jetsam, interior castles crumbling. This poor speaker—who knows what he's got in the bank—it's all drifting away from him now."

PATRICIA TRAXLER was born in San Diego, California, in 1947, and currently resides in Salina, Kansas, where she teaches creative writing at Kansas Wesleyan University. A Bunting Poetry Fellow at Radcliffe College from 1990 to 1992, she is the author of three volumes of poetry, most recently *Forbidden Words* (University of Missouri Press, 1994). Her earlier books were *Blood Calendar* (William Morrow, 1975) and *The Glass Woman* (Hanging Loose Press, 1983). She recently completed a novel, *Earthly Luck*, and a collection of short stories, *The Eternity Bird*. She received a 1992 Writer's Voice Award for short fiction and the 1990 Cohen Award for poetry from *Ploughshares*.

Traxler writes: "Although 'Death of a Distant In-law' is based on a real experience, the first line was all I put on paper at the time it occurred, and the image stayed with me for several years before I wrote the poem. It was during a long-term project teaching poetry to the deaf and hearing-impaired, for which I learned sign language, that I began thinking again about how locked away from the ordinary world the deaf can be when they have no access to the simplest conversations, to social small talk, word play, the subtle shadings of vocal intonation, and shared emotional confidences. It was then, when the language of signing brought me into their world in a new way, that the memory of this funeral and burial of a deaf and mute in-law renewed itself in me with some new urgency and clarity."

WILLIAM WADSWORTH was born in New York in 1950. He was educated at the University of Wisconsin and at Columbia. His poems have appeared in *Grand Street*, *The New Republic*, *Shenandoah*, *The Yale Review*, and *The Paris Review*. He is executive director of the Academy of American Poets in New York City.

Of "The Snake in the Garden Considers Daphne," Wadsworth writes: "The poem is about hands. It was inspired by a passage in W. H. Auden's essay, 'The Prolific and the Devourer.' Auden speculates that since humanity in some sense depends on the evolution of the opposable thumb, spiritual evolution depends on some kind of manipulation: of things, people, or ideas. The Snake and Daphne are parallel cases: two characters from two distinct mythologies, both of whom suffer the loss of their limbs and, in some sense, their humanity. The poem knocks them together; it is about lust on the one hand, salvation on the other."

KEVIN WALKER was born in Port Chester, New York, in 1964. He lives in Ann Arbor, Michigan, where he is on the staff of Food Gatherers, a nonprofit hunger relief agency. He also reviews books of poetry for the *Detroit Free Press*.

Of "My Talk with an Elegant Man," Walker writes: "This is one in a sequence of eleven-line poems I began when I didn't have time to write anything longer. I'd get home from work pretty worn out, but itching to try new poems. This eleven-line rule worked like a charm. It was dopey enough that it removed my inhibitions; it canceled out the urge to try to say something REALLY BIG. But at the same time the form encouraged a certain kind of daring: 'How much ground can I cover in so small a space?' That's why this poem happens so abruptly, plopping two characters down on its little stage with no introduction or explanation. I hope that their conversation touches on the tension between leisure and conscience."

ROSANNE WASSERMAN was born in Louisville, Kentucky, in 1952. She teaches at the U.S. Merchant Marine Academy in King's Point, New York. At Indiana University, Columbia University, and the Graduate Center of CUNY, she studied with Ruth Stone, David Ignatow, and Allen Mandelbaum. With her husband, the poet Eugene Richie, she operates the Groundwater Press, a nonprofit poetry publisher. Her latest books are *Apple Perfume* (Groundwater, 1989) and *The Lacemakers* (Gnosis 1992).

Of "Putting in a Word," Wasserman writes: "The 'you' who

begins this poem is a poet who once introduced me to a group of people as 'Eugene's *wife*,' putting a bitter edge on the word. The other 'yous' to whom the poem should be dedicated are: Eugene; Susie Wilson, late of Aughwich Mills, Pennsylvania, whom I will always miss: John Ashbery, who sent me back to look for that Morse-code scarf: Marilyn Robie, because of her voice laughing when she was seven or eight years old; Jeffrey Lewis Cohen, who was lost to AIDS not long ago; my mother, Jeanne, whom I 'sound just like' on the phone; and my brother Stan, who sat beside me on a plane from Urbana as I was writing this poem."

BRUCE WEIGL was born in Lorain, Ohio, in 1949. A Vietnam veteran, he saw action with the 1st Air Cav in 1967–68. He is the author of six collections of poetry, most recently *Song of Napalm* (Atlantic Monthly Press, 1988) and *What Saves Us* (TriQuarterly Books, 1992). He has served as editor or co-editor of three collections of critical essays, including *The Phenomenology of Spirit and Self: On the Poetry of Charles Simic* (forthcoming from Story Line Press). In 1994 the University of Massachusetts Press will publish *Poems from Captured Documents*, which he translated from the Vietnamese in collaboration with Nguyen Thanh. Weigl has taught at the University of Arkansas and at Old Dominion University, and currently directs the M.F.A. program in writing at Pennsylvania State University. He is a past president of the Associated Writing Programs.

Weigl writes: "I wrote 'The One' as part of a process of going back to my early life for a book in progress called *Sweet Lorain*, Lorain being the steel mill town in which I grew up and lived until I left for the war in 1967. In spite of its central focus—the beating of a child by his father with a belt—I don't think of the poem as an attack on the father. In those days, I must say, fathers beat their children, especially their boy children, in the working-class community of my childhood. I know there is a deeper pathology at work in the poem—that which the unconscious delivers to the page—but of course I didn't set out to narrate that. What saves the poem in my mind from being cruel or accusatory is what saves the boy of the poem from hating his father: the gesture of being taken into the lap of the father after the beating and being loved in whatever strange and convoluted 'office' that love may have existed. The poem is important to the story of *Sweet Lorain* for the way it illustrates plainly the paradox of my life in that town with those people during those days. The impossible beauty of the mill stacks and slag heaps. The rough-hewn love of those who would as soon slap you as kiss you on your lips. The fathers who didn't know what to do with their anger so passed it on to their sons. And most importantly how we manage somehow to survive that dark love, all of us."

JOSHUA WEINER was born in 1963. He grew up in Lawrenceville, New Jersey. A recipient of a "Discovery"/*The Nation* Award and the Joseph Henry Jackson Award from the San Francisco Foundation, Weiner was a 1993–94 fellow at the Fine Arts Work Center in Provincetown, Massachusetts.

Of "Who They Were," Weiner writes: "During a visit with my grandfather I realized that he was able to recognize neither my exact relation to him nor his relation to the figures of his parents hanging on the apartment wall. This incident disturbed and frightened me. I later felt a poem there and started to sketch something in blank verse, but got stuck until I read Book VIII of the *Aeneid*, where Aeneas accepts the shield from his mother and, not recognizing his ancestors engraved there by Vulcan, merely admires the depictions of their anonymous heroic deeds, slings the shield over his shoulder, and walks into battle. The connection seems to tell one part of a story of how flesh struggles into myth. The first part of 'Who They Were' tries to tell another. I chose iambic pentameter, one of the epic lines of English verse, because it sounded like the natural measure: by that I mean it contains a past music that remains alive in my ear and that seemed wedded to my subject, which concerns itself, in part, with history, lineage, and memory."

HENRY WEINFIELD was born in Montreal, Canada, in 1949. He teaches in the Program of Liberal Studies at the University of Notre Dame. He has published three chapbook collections of poetry: *The Carnival Cantata* (Unicorn Press, 1971), *In the Sweetness of the New Time* (House of Keys, 1980), and *Sonnets Elegiac and Satirical* (House of Keys, 1982). A critical study, *The Poet Without a Name: Gray's Elegy and the Problem of History*, was published by Southern Illinois University Press in 1991. He is completing *The Collected Poems of Stéphane Mallarmé*, a translation and commentary, to be published by the University of California Press in the fall of 1994.

Weinfield writes: "In 'Song for the In-Itself and For-Itself,' I borrow the terminology of Jean-Paul Sartre, who had adapted the 'in-itself' and 'for-itself' ('*en-soi*' and '*pour-soi*') pairing from the philosophy of G. W. F. Hegel. Part of the enjoyment I derived from writing this poem came from the fact that the word 'self' is very difficult to rhyme (which is probably a good thing, considering how narcissistic most poets are); and it was through the necessity of rhyming that the poem generated many of its details. I was especially pleased at being able to include the Ghibellines and the Guelphs in the poem, because of the grief these two groupings gave poor Dante. The Ghibellines were the party of the emperor, while the Guelphs were loyal to the papacy—except that eventually the Guelph party split into the Black Guelphs and the White Guelphs. They all came to blows, at various times and in various ways, and in this they demonstrate that they were essentially identical to each other (as the contemporary philosopher René Girard might say). The technique of personification has been in disrepute for about two hundred years, but in this poem I am aiming at the human condition—a subject on which, I am sorry to say, the poem does not manage to be very cheerful."

MICHAEL WHITE was born in Washington, D.C., in 1956. He grew up in Missouri, and after a four-year stint in the navy, was educated at the University of Missouri and the University of Utah. He has received fellowships from the National Endowment for the Arts and the Breadloaf Writers Conference, and currently teaches at the University of North Carolina at Wilmington. His books are *This Water*, which won the 1989 Silverfish Review Chapbook Competition, and *The Island*, published by Copper Canyon Press in 1992.

Of "*Camille Monet sur son lit de mort*," White notes: "I wrote this poem in August 1992, at Yaddo, the artists' colony in upstate New York. My wife had died of cancer eight months before, and I'd tried several times to write of that, but was beginning to think the experience was just too much for me. But sitting in my studio one afternoon, looking out over Yaddo's famous gardens (which must have been what brought Monet to mind), I vaguely remembered that Monet had painted a study of his first wife, who also died of cancer, in the moments following her death. The fact that he did this at all, and his meticulous, clinical devotion to the portrait— eerily unlike his other work—had been, later, a troubling memory for him. In any case, I saw the aesthetic parallels, and knew the painting might provide an approach. The next day I found a copy in a book in the Skidmore College library, and then did nothing for two days but stare at it, and at the Yaddo gardens, completely absorbed. When I had looked long enough, I began to write, and finished so quickly I mistrusted the poem for months afterward."

RICHARD WILBUR was born in New York City in 1921. An Amherst graduate, he "began to versify in earnest" during the Second World War, in which he saw action in Cassino and Anzio and along the Siegfried Line. His *New and Collected Poems*, published by Harcourt Brace Jovanovich in 1988, won the Pulitzer Prize. In 1987–88, he served as the nation's second official poet laureate, succeeding Robert Penn Warren. He recently published a book of verses and drawings, for children and others, called *More Opposites* (Harcourt Brace, 1991). A translation of Moliere's *School for Husbands* appeared from Harcourt in 1992; a paperback edition, also containing a one-act Moliere farce called *Sganarelle, or The Imaginary Cuckold*, is scheduled for 1994.

Of "A Digression," Wilbur writes: "An observant reader of *The New Yorker* wrote to ask if I hadn't had William James in mind when writing the fifth stanza. Yes, I had a vague, hovering recollection of James's oft-quoted description of the newborn infant's world: 'a blooming, buzzing confusion of pure sensation *sans* organization.'"

DEAN YOUNG was born in Columbia, Pennsylvania, in 1955. He has been a fellow at the Fine Arts Work Center at Provincetown and a Stegner Fellow at Stanford University. His two books of poems, *Design with X* (1988) and *Beloved Infidel* (1992), were both published by Wesleyan University Press. He teaches at Loyola University in Chicago.

Young writes: "After a night of not being able to reach a friend who I had heard had split with his wife, I wrote the first draft of this poem ['Upon Hearing of My Friend's Marriage Breaking Up'], incorporating a quotation from a radio interview with John L'Heureux. The poem, like many of my poems, is occasional—I find that the clarity of a particular situation gives me a firm launching point for lyrical gathering and exploration, quickly establishing, to some extent, the cause and/or justification of the jittery associations. Perhaps the humor comes from my own unease with both the certainty of my friend's suffering and my inability to help. But I hope the poem demonstrates some of the turmoil and emotional excess we are all so disastrously, and richly, capable of."

MAGAZINES WHERE THE POEMS
WERE FIRST PUBLISHED

Agni Review, ed. Askold Melnyczuk. Creative Writing Program, Boston University, 236 Bay State Road, Boston, MA 02215.

American Poetry Review, eds. Stephen Berg, David Bonanno, and Arthur Vogelsang. 1721 Walnut Street, Philadelphia, PA 19103.

Another Chicago Magazine, eds. Lee Webster and Barry Silesky. 3709 N. Kenmore, Chicago, IL 60613.

Ascent, ed. Audrey Curley. P.O. Box 967, Urbana, IL 61801.

The Beloit Poetry Journal, ed. Marion K. Stocking. Box 154, RFD 2 Ellsworth, ME 04605.

Boulevard, ed. Richard Burgin. P.O. Box 30386. Philadelphia, PA 19103.

The Bridge, poetry ed. Mitzi Alvin. 14050 Vernon St., Oak Park, MI 48237.

Callaloo, ed. Charles H. Rowell. University of Virginia, Department of English, Wilson Hall, Charlottesville, VA 22903.

Chelsea, ed. Sonia Raiziss. Box 5880, Grand Central Station, New York, NY 10163.

Colorado Review, poetry ed. Jorie Graham. 359 Eddy/Department of English, Colorado State University, Fort Collins, CO 80523.

Field, eds. Stuart Friebert and David Young. Rice Hall, Oberlin College, Oberlin, OH 44074.

Fine Madness, eds. Sean Bentley, Louis Bergsagel, Christine Deavel, John Malek, and John Marshall. P.O. Box 31138, Seattle, WA 98103.

The Gettysburg Review, ed. Peter Stitt. Gettysburg College, Gettysburg, PA 17325.

Glass Technology, ed. B. E. Moody. Society of Glass Technology, 20 Hallam Gate Road, Sheffield S10 5BT England.

Grand Street, ed. Jean Stein. 131 Varick St., Room 906, New York, NY 10013.

Green Mountains Review, ed. Neil Shepard. Johnson State College, Johnson, VT 05656.

The Hudson Review, eds. Paula Deitz and Frederick Morgan. 684 Park Avenue, New York, NY 10021.

The Iowa Review, ed. David Hamilton. 308 EPB, University of Iowa, Iowa City, IA 52242.

The Kenyon Review, ed. Marilyn Hacker. Kenyon College, Gambier, OH 43022.

Michigan Quarterly Review, ed. Laurence Goldstein. University of Michigan, 3032 Rackham Building, Ann Arbor, MI 48109.

The New Criterion, poetry ed. Robert Richman. 850 Seventh Avenue, New York, NY 10019.

New England Review, ed. T. R. Hummer. Middlebury College, Middlebury, VT 05753.

The New Republic, poetry ed. Mary Jo Salter. 1220 19th Street, NW, Washington, DC 20036.

The New York Review of Books, eds. Barbara Epstein and Robert Silvers. 250 West 57th Street, New York, NY 10107.

The New York Times, op-ed page ed. Mitchell Levitas. 229 West 43rd Street, New York, NY 10036.

The New Yorker, poetry ed. Alice Quinn. 20 West 43rd Street, New York, NY 10036.

No Roses Review, eds. San Juanita Garza, Natalie Kenvin, and Carolyn Koo. P.O. Box 597781, Chicago, IL 60659.

Northwest Review, poetry ed. John Witte. 369 P.L.C., University of Oregon, Eugene, OR 97403.

The Paris Review, poetry ed. Richard Howard. 541 East 72nd Street, New York, NY 10021.

Ploughshares, poetry ed. David Daniel. Emerson College, 100 Beacon Street, Boston, MA 02116.

Poet Lore, executive eds. Philip K. Jason and Barbara Goldberg. The Writer's Center, 7815 Old Georgetown Road, Bethesda, MD 20814.

Poetry, ed. Joseph Parisi. 60 West Walton Street, Chicago, IL 60610.

Poetry New York, eds. Cheryl Fish and Burt Kimmelman. P.O. Box 3184, Church Street Station, New York, NY 10008.

River Styx, ed. Lee Schreiner. 14 S. Euclid, St. Louis, MO 63108.

Salmagundi, ed. Robert Boyers. Skidmore College, Saratoga Springs, NY 12866.

Seneca Review, ed. Deborah Tall. Hobart and William Smith Colleges, Geneva, NY 14456.

Southwest Review, ed. Willard Spiegelman. Southern Methodist University, Dallas, TX 75275.

Tar River Poetry, ed. Peter Makuck. Department of English, East Carolina University, Greenville, NC 27858.

The Threepenny Review, ed. Wendy Lesser. P.O. Box 9131, Berkeley, CA 94709.

TriQuarterly, ed. Reginald Gibbons. Northwestern University, 2020 Ridge Avenue, Evanston, IL 60208.

Urbanus, ed. Peter Drizhal. P.O. Box 192561, San Francisco, CA 94119.

Witness, ed. Peter Stine. Oakland Community College, Orchard Ridge Campus, 27055 Orchard Lake Road, Farmington Hills, MI 48334.

The Yale Review, ed. J. D. McClatchy. P.O. Box 1902A, Yale Station, New Haven, CT 06520.

ZYZZYVA, ed. Howard Junker. 41 Sutter, Suite 1400, San Francisco, CA 94104.

ACKNOWLEDGMENTS

The series editor wishes to thank his assistant, Kate Fox Reynolds, as well as Glen Hartley and Lynn Chu of Writers' Representatives, Inc., and Hamilton Cain, Sharon Dynak, and Barbara Grossman of Charles Scribner's Sons.

Grateful acknowledgment is made to the publications from which the poems in this volume were chosen. Unless specifically noted otherwise, copyright of the poems is held by the individual poets.

Dick Allen: "A Short History of the Vietnam War Years" appeared in *The Gettysburg Review*. Reprinted by permission of the poet.

Tom Andrews: "Cinema Vérité" appeared in *Field*. Reprinted by permission of the poet.

John Ashbery: "Myrtle" from *And The Stars Were Shining* by John Ashbery. Copyright © 1994 John Ashbery. Reprinted by permission of the poet and of Farrar, Straus & Giroux. The poem initially appeared in *The New Yorker*, March 15, 1993.

Burlin Barr: "Tremendous Mood Swings" appeared in *Grand Street*. Reprinted by permission of the poet.

Cynthia Bond: "What You Want Means What You Can Afford" appeared in *Ascent*. Reprinted by permission of the poet.

Catherine Bowman: "Demographics" from *1-800-HOT-RIBS* (Peregrine Smith). Copyright © 1993 by Catherine Bowman. Reprinted by permission. The poem first appeared in *TriQuarterly*.

George Bradley: "The Fire Fetched Down" appeared in *The Paris Review*. Reprinted by permission of the poet.

Charles Bukowski: "me against the world" appeared in *Urbanus*. Reprinted by permission of the poet and of Black Sparrow Press.

Rebecca Byrkit: "The Only Dance There Is" appeared in *New England Review*. Reprinted by permission of the poet.

Amy Clampitt: "A Catalpa Tree on West Twelfth Street" appeared in *The New York Times*, op-ed page (June 21, 1993). Reprinted by permission.

Michelle T. Clinton: "Tantrum Girl Responds to Death" appeared in *The Kenyon Review* and in *Good Sense and The Faithless* (West End Press, 1994). Reprinted by permission of the poet.

James Cummins: "Sestina" appeared in *The Paris Review*. Reprinted by permission of the poet.

Ramola Dharmaraj: "full of rain, the word" appeared in *Green Mountains Review*. Reprinted by permission of the poet.

Thomas M. Disch: "The Cardinal Detoxes" appeared in *The Hudson Review*. Reprinted by permission.

CUMULATIVE SERIES INDEX

The following are the annual listings in alphabetical order of poets and poems reprinted in the first six editions of *The Best American Poetry*

1990
Edited and Introduced by Jorie Graham

1991
Edited and Introduced by Mark Strand

1992
Edited and Introduced by Charles Simic

1993
Edited and Introduced by Louise Glück

ALSO AVAILABLE FROM
THE BEST AMERICAN POETRY SERIES